MANIFEST DESTINY

MILESTONES

IN

AMERICAN HISTORY

MANIFEST DESTINY

WESTWARD EXPANSION

S HANE M OUNTJOY

CHELSEA HOUSE
PUBLISHERS
An imprint of Infobase Publishing

Manifest Destiny

Copyright © 2009 by Infobase Publishing

Chelsea House
An imprint of Infobase Publishing
132 West 31st Street
New York NY 10001

Library of Congress Cataloging-in-Publication Data

Mountjoy, Shane, 1967–
  Manifest destiny : westward Expansion / Shane Mountjoy.
    p. cm.—(Milestones in American history)
  Includes bibliographical references and index.
  ISBN 978-1-60413-055-3 (hardcover)
  1. United States—Territorial expansion—Juvenile literature. 2. West (U.S.)—Discovery and exploration—Juvenile literature. 3. West (U.S.)—History—19th century—Juvenile literature. I. Title. II. Series.
  E179.5.M685 2009
  973—dc22   2008030744

Chelsea House books are available at special discounts when purchased in bulk quantities for businesses, associations, institutions, or sales promotions. Please call our Special Sales Department in New York at (212) 967-8800 or (800) 322-8755.

You can find Chelsea House on the World Wide Web at http://www.chelseahouse.com

Series design by Erik Lindstrom
Cover design by Ben Peterson

Printed in the United States of America

Bang NMSG 10 9 8 7 6 5 4 3 2 1

This book is printed on acid-free paper.

All links and Web addresses were checked and verified to be correct at the time of publication. Because of the dynamic nature of the Web, some addresses and links may have changed since publication and may no longer be valid.

CONTENTS

A Barnburner

David Wilmot sat at the table with several other members of Congress. The group had held regular meetings for weeks, trying to formulate a strategy that would challenge the administration of President James K. Polk and its apparent war policy. The men at the table believed that they needed to do something to shift the debate to the important issue of slavery. Wilmot looked at the face of each man and reflected. He thought about the direction the United States seemed to be taking. He worried that Southern states held too much power within the federal government. He had become convinced, as had the others at the table, that those same Southern states exercised their power to protect and expand slavery. He wondered what was becoming of the America he knew.

Wilmot sat quietly, listening and watching his companions. Soon, he began to think of his own life. He thought of his father, a wealthy merchant from Bethany, Pennsylvania. Born in 1814, Wilmot always had enjoyed the benefits of his family's wealth. He attended private academies and began to study law in 1832. In 1834, he gained admittance to the Pennsylvania bar. Two years later, he married Anna Morgan. Although the young couple had three children, none survived to adulthood. Wilmot practiced law in Towanda, Pennsylvania, where he involved himself in local politics by supporting Andrew Jackson. In 1844, the 30-year-old lawyer ran as a Democrat and won election to the U.S. House of Representatives.

Now he sat with other members of the House, discussing the war with Mexico and its impact on the nation. Critics had labeled the other members of the group with the name Barnburner Democrats. These so-called barnburners represented the more radical element of the Democratic Party, especially in the state of New York. Critics within the party insisted that those who were against slavery were so focused on their opposition to that practice that the party would suffer as a result. The term *barnburner* came from the mental picture of a farmer trying to rid himself of a rat by burning down his barn.

Many Democrats believed that barnburner efforts would destroy the party. Other Democrats claimed the name with pride. One Democratic radical who apparently liked the word picture stated, "Gentlemen, they call us barnburners. Thunder and lightning are barnburners sometimes; but they greatly purify the whole atmosphere, and that, gentlemen, is what we propose to do."[1] Most Democrats viewed the other congressional strategists meeting with Wilmot as barnburners.

Wilmot's record concealed his growing distrust of Southern power and influence, however. The Pennsylvania representative had offered strong support for Polk and his policies. Wilmot also counted many Southerners as close friends. The barnburner group looked to Wilmot as the one at the table most likely to be granted some time to speak on the floor of

David Wilmot (1814–1868), a representative and senator from Pennsylvania, sponsored the Wilmot Proviso, which opposed the expansion of slavery into any territory acquired from Mexico. He also helped to found the Republican Party.

the House. Because House leaders viewed the other barnburners with suspicion, there was little chance that they would be allowed to enter into the debate.

On Saturday, August 8, 1846, President Polk submitted an appropriations request to Congress for $2 million. The president wanted the money to fund negotiations with Mexico at the close of the war that the United States was fighting against its North American neighbor. The president's move was both premature and shortsighted. The war with Mexico was only three months old. The United States had not yet won the war and was not close to doing so. Mexico showed no willingness to compromise or negotiate an end to the conflict. Instead, America's southern neighbor had consistently stated its intention to continue fighting. In view of these circumstances, a presidential request for funding to conclude negotiations seemed somewhat hasty. In contrast, an amendment to the president's bill painted a picture of what the results of the war might possibly be—a victorious United States with an additional nonslave territory.

The request was shortsighted because Polk assumed that Congress would pass the bill quickly. Instead, the submission of the appropriations bill allowed opponents of the war to challenge the validity of the conflict with Mexico and the president's policy toward any territory won. House leaders, sensing no opposition to an apparently safe bill, introduced the request in a special night session. No individual was allowed to speak for more than 10 minutes, and all debate was limited to two hours. Wilmot was included in the debate schedule, and he offered an amendment to the spending bill that would carry his name.

The Wilmot Proviso was concise and to the point: It contained only 71 words. It was patterned after the Northwest Ordinance of 1787. In his proviso, Wilmot offered the following:

> Provided, That, as an express and fundamental condition to the acquisition of any territory from the Republic of Mexico by the United States, by virtue of any treaty which may be negotiated between them, and to the use by the Executive of the moneys herein appropriated, neither slavery nor

involuntary servitude shall ever exist in any part of said territory, except for crime, whereof the party shall first be duly
convicted.[2]

Despite its brevity, Wilmot's amendment stirred up passions in the hearts of supporters and opponents like nothing
before it. Opposition to the proviso resulted in the proposal of
another amendment that aimed to extend the slavery restrictions of the earlier Missouri Compromise in 1820 to the Pacific
Ocean. Many Southerners believed that the Wilmot Proviso
confirmed their fears of Northern conspiracies to destroy
slavery. Other Southerners believed that the proviso stemmed
from Northern arrogance and condescension toward Southern culture. Historian William W. Freehling writes that "Most
Southerners raged primarily because David Wilmot's holierthan-thou stance was so insulting."[3]

The opposing amendment failed, leaving the House to vote
on the Wilmot Proviso. The House passed the proviso and
added it to the president's request for funds. Southern representatives then employed a parliamentary tactic: They proposed to
table, or postpone, the entire spending bill. The House voted
against the proposal to postpone and then narrowly approved
the complete appropriations bill. The final vote demonstrated
the growing rift within the United States: Sectional divisions
were more indicative of votes than were party affiliations.

The appropriations bill moved on to the Senate, where
Democrats voted down Wilmot's amendment and removed
any restrictions on slavery in the future. A senator who was
a member of the Whig party and who supported Wilmot's
amendment intended to stall long enough to compel the Senate
to vote on the measure with the proviso included. The clocks in
the two congressional chambers were not synchronized, however, and the House adjourned before the Senate could send the
bill back to the House for reconsideration. The special night
session ended without Congress passing the spending bill.

This 1850 cartoon attacks abolitionists, Free-Soil, and other sectionalist interests as dangers to the Union. The artist singles out (from left to right) Free-Soil advocate David Wilmot, abolitionist William Lloyd Garrison, Southern states' rights spokesman John Calhoun, and newspaper editor Horace Greeley for placing their concerns above the Union's interests. The men wearing fools' caps add sacks marked with their various issues into the hurly-burly pot while military traitor Benedict Arnold reaches out from the flames.

Polk rekindled the debate in his annual message to Congress at the end of 1846, when he again asked for money to negotiate the end of the war. He raised the amount to $3 million and attempted to explain and justify his request. The president insisted that the United States had not entered into war with Mexico to win territory but to defend the nation's boundary. Any honorable peace would no doubt include some compensation to the United States, however, and territory would be included in such compensation. [4]

The House considered nothing other than the so-called Three Million Dollar Bill for a full week in February 1847. Representative Preston King of New York, one of the barnburners who had met with Wilmot, reintroduced an expanded Wilmot Proviso. This time, the amendment extended slavery restrictions to "any territory on the continent of America which shall hereafter be acquired." [5] Again, some House members offered a counterproposal to extend the Missouri Compromise line of latitude 36°30' to extend west to the Pacific. The proposal was defeated. The House again passed the proviso before sending the bill to the Senate, where the proviso failed to pass. The House ended up adopting the Senate version of the bill, even though every Northern Whig in the House voted in favor of keeping the proviso. For the time being, partisan loyalties carried the day: More than 20 of the House's Northern Democrats voted against reinserting the proviso.

The Wilmot Proviso never went away. When President Polk sent the Treaty of Guadalupe Hidalgo (the peace treaty that brought an end to the Mexican-American War) to the Senate for ratification, slavery opponents attempted to include the proviso as an amendment. Others proposed their own solutions to the slavery issue. In 1848, Democratic presidential nominee Lewis Cass offered this alternative to the Wilmot Proviso: "Leave it to the people, who will be affected by this question to adjust it upon their own responsibility, and in their own manner, and we shall render another tribute to the original principles of our government, and furnish another for its permanence and prosperity." [6] Even though the Wilmot Proviso failed, its ideal continued to shape the political landscape.

Another Democrat, Stephen A. Douglas of Illinois, adopted Cass's idea and called it "popular sovereignty." Douglas believed that local residents, not the federal government, should decide the issue of slavery. He also insisted that any debate concerning slavery in the territories should take place only after Congress organized a territory and established a territorial government.

Otherwise, according to Douglas, all discussion was rash and subject to too many hypothetical conditions.

David Wilmot's proposal initiated a national debate and is considered one of the first events that eventually resulted in the Civil War. When the Pennsylvania congressman put forward his proviso, he did so to help his country. The controversy that surrounded the Wilmot Proviso demonstrates the importance of the issue of slavery. It was, however, another philosophy and accompanying set of ideals that launched slavery to the forefront of American politics. That philosophy was Manifest Destiny.

The Origins of Manifest Destiny

The phrase *Manifest Destiny* is used to express the belief that it was the fate of the United States to expand across the American continent. The idea of Manifest Destiny was not new to America in the 1840s. The term itself did not appear, however, until an editor named John O'Sullivan used it to describe his dream of America's future. Many people credit O'Sullivan with coining the term when it first appeared in a journal that he cofounded, *The United States Magazine and Democratic Review*. The term symbolized the ideology and desire for the United States to expand.

O'Sullivan published an essay called "Annexation" in the July-August 1845 issue of the *Democratic Review*. In the essay, which O'Sullivan wrote, he voiced support for the American acquisition of Texas. In 1845 Texas was an independent republic that wanted to join the Union. According to O'Sullivan, it was the "fulfillment of our manifest destiny to overspread the continent allotted by Providence for the free development of our yearly multiplying millions."[1] The annexation of Texas went forward, but O'Sullivan's first use of the term *Manifest Destiny* went virtually unnoticed.

Later that year, in the December 27 issue of the *New York Morning News*, O'Sullivan again used the term *Manifest Destiny* to explain his view about another matter having to do with the annexation of western territory. This time, the land in question was Oregon. O'Sullivan maintained that the United States had rights to all of Oregon. O'Sullivan then declared that this "claim is by the right of our manifest destiny to overspread and possess the whole of the continent which Providence has given us for the development of the great experiment of liberty and federated self-government entrusted to us."[2] In short, O'Sullivan argued that Providence, the eighteenth and nineteenth century term for God, had ordained the United States to extend its unique and relatively new form of government, the so-called "great experiment of liberty and federated self-government."[3] According to this view, because Great Britain was the primary competitor for Oregon and Great Britain's form of government included a monarchy, the new American traditions of government outweighed British claims. Ironically, O'Sullivan's view seemed to mirror the views of the supporters of so-called divine-right monarchs, who claimed God's ordination of those monarchs' rights. O'Sullivan felt that America's Manifest Destiny embodied a higher law—God's law—and so held the moral high ground over Britain's claims to Oregon.[4]

Despite these beliefs, O'Sullivan did not advocate gaining territory through the use of force. Instead, he favored a gradual enlargement of the United States through settlement. O'Sullivan believed that in their communities, these settlers would naturally establish institutions of government that copied the American model of republican government. Such communities and governments would no doubt desire to enter into the Union, as Texas had done. O'Sullivan trusted that

In Frances Palmer's *Across the Continent: Westward the Course of Empire Takes Its Way* (1868) American westward expansion is idealized. The painting shows a train traveling to the Pacific toward the open prairie while leaving a pair of American Indians literally in its smoke, as hearty pioneers nurture and civilize the land. The rushing locomotive and the men erecting telegraph poles along the tracks represent the extension of the empire and taming of the wilderness, which many believed was the right and mission of the United States.

future territories, such as California, and existing governments, such as that of Canada, would eventually enter the Union. O'Sullivan did not foresee the use of the concept of Manifest Destiny to justify American expansion through war, as some people did during the Mexican-American War. Author William Earl Weeks notes, "It appeared to be America's sacred duty to expand across the North American continent, to reign supreme in the Western Hemisphere, and to serve as an example of the future to people everywhere. This was the Manifest Destiny of the American people."[5]

The third time O'Sullivan used the term *Manifest Destiny*, it was almost immediately picked up and adopted by others. Democrats were the first to use the term extensively. The phrase was a brief way to express support for American expansion and the annexation of western lands. The acquisition of these lands came at the expense of Great Britain and, especially, Mexico. These lands make up much of the modern-day western United States. In particular, as mentioned, the areas eyed for American expansion included Texas and Oregon. When the United States entered into a war with Mexico, the supporters of Manifest Destiny sought to gain other territories, such as New Mexico and California.

Promoters of expansion used the term, which clearly stated their view of America's spreading out. To such people, American expansion and entitlement to western lands was obvious, or manifest. Because such expansion was sure to happen, it was America's destiny. The term *Manifest Destiny* came to embody all the hopes and expectations of expansionists in nineteenth-century America. Proponents of western expansion used the ideology of Manifest Destiny to defend the annexation of Texas, to defend support for resolving the Oregon dispute, and to defend the declaration of war with Mexico in 1846.

THE MEANING OF MANIFEST DESTINY

At the least, Manifest Destiny "meant expansion, prearranged by Heaven, over an area not clearly defined."[6] Other points of view saw Manifest Destiny as the right for the United States to gain land all the way to the Pacific Ocean. Still others enlarged the view to include all of North America, or even the entire Western Hemisphere. Regardless of the interpretation, the concept of Manifest Destiny spurred a political movement in the 1840s. The ideals of expansionism captured the nation, resulting in war with Mexico and an American Indian policy that virtually destroyed the culture of the continent's original inhabitants.

In practical terms, the United States did not adopt Manifest Destiny as a policy. Instead, the concept of Manifest Destiny influenced U.S. policy, especially in the last six decades of the nineteenth century. The term encompassed several beliefs. These were expansionism, nationalism, American exceptionalism, and, in some cases, the idea of racial superiority. Historian Ernest Lee Tuveson summarized the assortment of views this way: "A vast complex of ideas, policies, and actions is comprehended under the phrase 'Manifest Destiny.' They are not, as we should expect, all compatible, nor do they come from any one source."[7] Despite these complexities, the idea of Manifest Destiny generally meant that Americans and their government were certain to gain ownership of and establish political control over much of North America, and that their country would stretch from the Atlantic Ocean to the Pacific.

To its proponents, the idea of Manifest Destiny contained three identifiable themes: "the special virtues of the American people and their institutions; their mission to redeem and remake the world in the image of America; and the American destiny under God to accomplish this sublime task."[8] These elements are evident in O'Sullivan's words. Expansionists of the 1840s and 1850s believed in the rightness of the American way of life. They recognized the unique place and time in which they lived—a time and place that allowed them to expand the United States. They also were convinced of the certainty of their success. These beliefs make up the fundamental spirit of Manifest Destiny.

John O'Sullivan argued "that God had granted Americans use of the North American continent."[9] He held that "The inherent virtues of agrarianism, American entrepreneurship, republican institutions, and a conviction that European countries would eventually retreat from North America reinforced the idea that the United States would extend its superior civilization throughout the continent."[10] Such conditions would open the door for the United States to claim her rightful place as the continental power.

Supporters usually included three key concepts in their arguments for Manifest Destiny: virtue, mission, and destiny.[11] First, American society and citizens were virtuous. Because of their virtue, they were justified in expanding. Second, it was the mission of Americans to extend their society. In doing this, Americans would influence the rest of the world. Finally, it was the destiny of America to undertake the task of accomplishing these things. Each of these key concepts is evident in the politically charged discussions of American expansion during the 1840s and 1850s. "Manifest Destiny implied not simply territorial growth, but sanctified ideology and institutions."[12]

THE ROOTS OF MANIFEST DESTINY

The ideals contained within the concept of Manifest Destiny were certainly not novel. In 1820, in a speech commemorating the 200th anniversary of the founding of the Plymouth Colony, American statesman and orator Daniel Webster foresaw a grand future for the American people. Webster believed that the United States was certain to grow and that "[t]here is nothing to check them till they touch the shores of the Pacific, and then, they are so much accustomed to water, that *that's* a facility, and no obstruction!"[13]

Indeed, in 1630, an early Puritan leader named John Winthrop described the Massachusetts Bay Colony "as a city upon a hill."[14] This city on a hill was to serve as an example for all humankind, for all time. Winthrop also said "The eyes of all people are upon us."[15] The Puritan leader believed that God blessed the actions of the Pilgrims of the Plymouth Colony and the Puritan immigrants who followed them to America. Winthrop wanted his people's actions to be worthy of their beliefs. To this end, many of the early Massachusetts settlers believed that the institutions they established, the society they designed, and the lives they led laid the foundation for this city on a hill.

Political philosopher Thomas Paine argued for American independence from Great Britain in his 1776 tract *Common Sense*. Paine also saw the opportunity for Americans to influence the future of the world. In *Common Sense*, Paine wrote, "We have it in our power to begin the world over again."[16] The radical writer also foresaw the numeric growth of America, saying, "The birthday of a new world is at hand, and a race of men, perhaps as numerous as all Europe contains."[17] Many Americans reached the conclusion that their new nation needed to shed the trappings of European governments. The New World needed a new approach to government. Soon, as Paine encouraged and predicted, Americans won their independence, and their population began to increase rapidly during the nineteenth century. This growth fed the desire to expand the new nation's territorial holdings across the continent.

Although the basic idea was present earlier, the full-bodied ideal of Manifest Destiny did not take hold until the 1840s. By then, the United States had charted its course as a nation that sought to expand its territorial holdings by moving west. At the close of the Revolutionary War, Americans looked longingly to the Mississippi River. In the 1783 peace treaty that ended the war, Great Britain recognized the Mississippi as the western boundary of the newly formed United States of America. In 1803, the Louisiana Purchase extended the western limits of the United States well beyond the Mississippi, across the Great Plains. Interest in Oregon, California, and other places west of the Great Plains reflected a pattern of U.S. citizens migrating westward across the continent. Thus, "the habit of moving toward the western horizon became a fixed constant in the American chronicle."[18]

This westward movement was not altogether new. Early American leaders believed in the inevitable westward expansion of the young republic. John Quincy Adams, writing to his father, John Adams, in 1811, claimed,

Thomas Paine (1737–1809), an English intellectual, emigrated to the American colonies just before the American Revolution. He wrote the widely read pamphlet *Common Sense* promoting radical democracy and the ideals of American greatness and expansion, both of which were elements in Manifest Destiny.

North America appears to be destined by Divine Providence to be peopled by one nation, speaking one language, professing one general system of religious and political principles, and accustomed to one general tenor of social usages and customs. For the common happiness of them all, for their peace and prosperity, I believe it is indispensable that they should be associated in one federal Union."[19]

Clearly, John Quincy Adams viewed the English language, predominant American religious beliefs, political philosophies, and American culture as the means by which his people would pave the road westward to create an expanded American nation.

The ideal of Manifest Destiny symbolized one way that Americans saw the world and their role in it. Americans also wanted to explain, in rational terms, their aims to secure the continent. "Manifest Destiny, in essence, was a philosophy to explain and justify expansionism both to Europeans, who viewed American aggrandizement with alarm, and to the American people themselves, who needed reassurance that the course was righteous."[20]

ADAPTING MANIFEST DESTINY

Some people altered the purpose of Manifest Destiny to meet their changing vision of the United States. Some people saw expansion as the only way to preserve a way of life. The idea of expanding American culture through territorial expansion was always a part of Manifest Destiny. In the 1840s and 1850s, Southerners seized on this concept and claimed it as a way to protect the institution of slavery. As historian Reginald Stuart has put it, "Southerners wanted new land because they believed that slavery must expand or else shrivel and die."[21] Southerners believed that the United States needed to acquire more territory for the South to maintain its distinctive society. Historian Albert K. Weinberg maintains, "The Southern States held Texas to be necessary to their economic prosperity, the security of their 'peculiar institution,' and their maintenance of a balance of political power with the North."[22] The South "defended this institution on cultural as well as economic and constitutional grounds" to preserve their regional culture.[23]

When the issue of Texas annexation arose, the question of expansion centered on forward progress versus backward thinking. "Whereas it had once been feared that the existence of the Union was jeopardized by expansion, it was now apprehended that the Union might be [imperiled] by failure to expand through annexing Texas."[24] In the opinion of many people in the South, if the United States did not annex Texas, civil war was sure to follow.

Annexation also provided the South with opportunities to increase the amount of congressional representation for states where slavery was legal. One Southern representative described the political reality facing the South: "Every census has added to the power of the non-slaveholding States, and diminished that of the South. We are growing weaker, and they stronger, every day."[25] Unless the South gained additional slave states, the ability to maintain the region's power in the federal government became a matter of simple arithmetic. Without expansion, the destiny of the South appeared to be little more than that of a perpetual minority party.

Southerners who supported the extension of slavery did not choose to cloak their arguments in the mantle of Manifest Destiny purely by accident. Instead, many Southerners realized that the aura of Manifest Destiny was both captivating and powerful. Much of the term's power stems from its strong bonds to American nationalism: "Under the aegis of virtue, mission, and destiny evolved a powerful nationalist mythology that was virtually impossible to oppose and, for many, almost without an alternative."[26] As such, Manifest Destiny was as much a patriotic ideal as it was a term. National politics were tumultuous in the 1850s. The fact that the underlying justification for the expansion of slavery was so uniquely American helps to explain this turmoil.

AMERICAN PROGRESS

Perhaps the best-known nineteenth century image of Manifest Destiny is an 1872 painting by John Gast called *American Progress*. In this allegorical painting, Gast portrays America "as a light-haired woman, classically dressed, who is leading the Americans west."* The portrayal resembles similar depictions of the ideals of liberty or justice. The scene shows American civilization and industry in the East. The figure of America, who has the "star of empire" on her forehead, is shown heading westward, leading pioneers, farmers, miners, wagons, and railroads.** The westward movement drives out American Indians and buffalo. The figure of America also carries a book that represents learning and knowledge, and she strings the wire of the telegraph as she goes. This painting illustrates the view "that American conquest of the west was a sign of progress, taking civilization and prosperity to unenlightened peoples."*** *American Progress* is a revealing and unforgettable depiction of American Manifest Destiny.

---

* George A. Crofutt. American Progress. *Available online at http://memory.loc.gov/ammem/awhhtml/aw06e/d10.html.*
** Amy S. Greenberg. Manifest Manhood and the Antebellum American Empire. *New York: Cambridge University Press, 2005. Also available online at http://assets.cambridge.org/97805218/40965/excerpt/9780521840965_excerpt.pdf.*
*** Crofutt.

LATER USE OF MANIFEST DESTINY

The power and success of Manifest Destiny as a way to convey American ideals led to the concept's use in later years. In the 1890s, the term *Manifest Destiny* resurfaced. Again, the phrase symbolized Americans' desire to expand their territorial holdings. This time, however, Manifest Destiny was used to defend American expansion outside North America. Specifically, some people wanted to establish the United States as a world power by gaining colonies. In 1898, the Spanish-American War provided such an opportunity. In the aftermath of the war, the United States found itself the proud owner of the islands of the Philippines, Puerto Rico, and Guam. The United States also asserted power over Cuba, playing the role of a protector of Cuban independence.

Few Americans in the twentieth century continued to use Manifest Destiny to describe their policy goals. Other terms emerged, however, and several of these carried some of the same ideas. Specifically, the concept that America needed to lead the free world as part of its mission contained many of the ideals of Manifest Destiny. Consistent with Manifest Destiny, these later ideals tied policy initiatives and aims to national pride and to the role of America as a world power. At the very least, later manifestations of Manifest Destiny exemplified the spirit of John O'Sullivan's term.

The Early Republic Looks West

The Treaty of Paris of 1783 ended the American Revolution. Under the terms of this agreement, Great Britain recognized her former colonies as a sovereign and independent nation. In addition, Great Britain ceded control of lands south of the Great Lakes and east of the Mississippi to the United States. Spain, one of America's allies in the war, received Florida, which the British had seized from the Spanish during the Seven Years' War and had kept after that conflict. Although the French had helped the Americans immensely during the Revolution, France received nothing. Great Britain, Spain, and the United States were the sole powers remaining in North America in 1783.

Fortunately for the United States, Spain was in decline and faced rising turmoil in its American colonies. Thus, Spain was the weakest of all the nations that held land desired by

Americans. In 1783, Spain held Florida and virtually all of the land west of the Mississippi River and south of present-day Washington and Oregon. Because Spain's status as a world power was waning, however, the young American nation stood a good chance of expanding its holdings at the expense of Spain.

Despite its declining power, Spain still could inhibit the growth of the new nation. President George Washington recognized the dangers of a foreign power (Spain) holding the city of New Orleans, Louisiana. That port, at the southern entrance to the Mississippi River, was the crucial entry point for waterborne trade with settlers in the western portions of the United States. To counter a possible threat from the Spanish at New Orleans, Washington authorized negotiations with Spain. These diplomatic talks resulted, in 1795, in the Treaty of San Lorenzo, which is also called Pinckney's Treaty. This agreement defined the boundaries between the United States and Spain's North American holdings and assured American access to the Gulf of Mexico. Specifically, Spain guaranteed the United States full navigation rights on the Mississippi River. The two countries pledged to respect each other's rights along the entire length of the river, including at the port of New Orleans. The two sides also agreed on a boundary between Florida and the United States, a border that is the present-day boundary between the states of Georgia and Florida. At the time of Pinckney's Treaty, the boundary also extended westward to the Mississippi River.

THE LOUISIANA PURCHASE

In 1803, the United States was a young nation perched on the eastern edge of the vast North American continent. Thomas Jefferson was the president. Jefferson believed in limited government and was convinced that government officials could act only in the ways that the Constitution specified. In an effort not to appear overly ambitious or politically aggressive, Jefferson exercised his executive powers with restraint. To Jefferson, to go beyond the Constitution was to raise the possibility of the government's abusing its power over its citizens. Despite his convictions on the powers and role of the government, however, Jefferson soon took advantage of an opportunity to expand the holdings of the United States in North America. To do this, Jefferson had to ignore the Constitution on the matter of purchasing territory from foreign powers.

Jefferson believed that the western lands held the key to a developing nation. He wrote to Robert Livingston, the American representative to France, that whoever held New Orleans was America's "natural and habitual enemy."[1] Jefferson loved France, having served there as the American minister from 1785 to 1789. Jefferson understood the dangers of France's holding lands west of the United States, however. If France took control of Louisiana, American interests would collide with French interests. As Jefferson put it to a friend, "The day that France takes possession of New Orleans, fixes the sentence which is to restrain her for ever within her low-water mark. It seals the union of two nations, who, in conjunction, can maintain exclusive possession of the ocean. From that moment we must marry ourselves to the British fleet and nation."[2] Given his distrust of Great Britain and his love for France, it must have been difficult for Jefferson to reach this conclusion.

As a lover of France and a lover of peace, Jefferson decided to act sooner rather than later. He dispatched representatives to France in an effort to purchase New Orleans. Then, without warning, the entire situation changed. France offered to sell not only New Orleans but also the whole of the Louisiana Territory to the United States. France once had held Louisiana but had surrendered it to Spain at the conclusion of the Seven Years' War (also called the French and Indian War) in 1763. Under the leadership of First Consul Napoleon Bonaparte, France pressured Spain to give Louisiana back under the terms of the Treaty of San Ildefonso in 1800. Napoleon insisted that the terms of the treaty remain secret, as France was unable to take possession of its former territory.

Realizing that another war with Great Britain was imminent, Napoleon decided that he no longer needed Louisiana. He offered to sell the territory to the United States. President Jefferson immediately recognized the value of this offer. In fact, his appreciation for the worth of the territory predated Napoleon's generous offer. In anticipation of purchasing New Orleans, the American president already had commissioned Meriwether Lewis and William Clark to explore the vast American West. Preparations for the Lewis and Clark expedition were under way before word reached the United States that France had sold Louisiana.

France sold the Louisiana Territory to the United States for about $15 million—a cost of about 4 cents per acre. The territory purchased was 828,000 square miles of land west of the Mississippi River. The size and boundaries of Louisiana were somewhat undefined. Robert Livingston asked French foreign minister Charles-Maurice de Talleyrand for detailed borders, but the Frenchman replied, "I can give you no direction. You have made a noble bargain for yourselves and I suppose you will make the most of it."[3] Land from the Louisiana Purchase that later was incorporated into states includes nearly a quarter of current U.S. territory. At the time of the purchase, it doubled the geographical size of the United States.

Despite his fears of the abuse of executive powers and the lack of constitutional authority to purchase land, President Jefferson acted without the consent of Congress. Worries about France, Spain, or Great Britain controlling the strategic city

The Louisiana Purchase Treaty, which was signed on April 30, 1803, expanded the United States by 800,000 square miles, from the Mississippi River to the Rocky Mountains. Some feared that the political power in the East would be threatened by the new citizens of the West, and that an increase in slave-holding states created out of the new territory would intensify divisions between North and South.

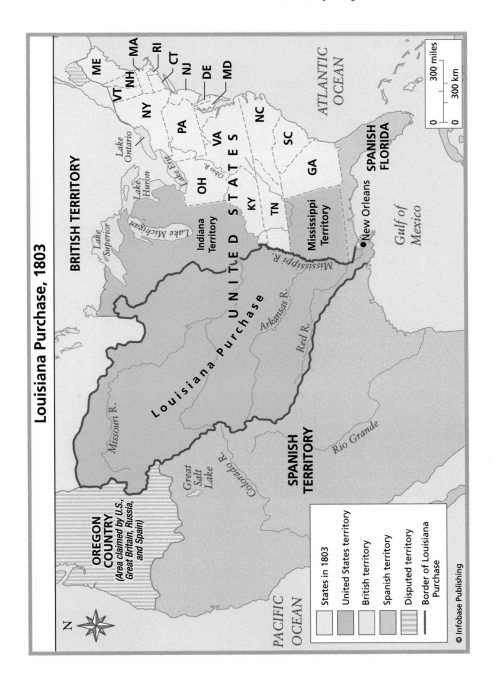

Louisiana Purchase, 1803

BRITISH TERRITORY

OREGON COUNTRY
(Area claimed by U.S., Great Britain, Russia, and Spain)

PACIFIC OCEAN

SPANISH TERRITORY

Great Salt Lake

Colorado R.

Rio Grande

Missouri R.

Louisiana Purchase

Arkansas R.

Red R.

UNITED STATES

Indiana Territory

Lake Superior

Lake Michigan

Lake Huron

Lake Erie

Lake Ontario

NY
PA
OH
KY
TN
VA
NC
SC
GA

Ohio R.

Mississippi R.

ME
VT
NH
MA
RI
CT
NJ
DE
MD

Mississippi Territory

New Orleans

SPANISH FLORIDA

Gulf of Mexico

ATLANTIC OCEAN

N

States in 1803
United States territory
British territory
Spanish territory
Disputed territory
Border of Louisiana Purchase

300 miles
300 km

© Infobase Publishing

of New Orleans, with its vital access to global trade, prompted Jefferson to act. The nation's third president did not want to see the growth of his country limited by a foreign power's holding New Orleans. He signed the treaty with France and sought approval after the fact. In doing this, Jefferson set a precedent for later presidents who thought that it sometimes is easier to receive forgiveness after taking an action than it is to obtain permission before that action. Jefferson's critics spoke out harshly against him, but the Republican Congress ratified the treaty and the United States doubled in size. Ultimately, Jefferson rationalized the purchase by claiming that "the laws of necessity, of self-preservation, of saving our country when in danger" demanded the unprecedented action.[4]

One obstacle remained before the United States could gain possession of Louisiana. Although France technically owned Louisiana, Napoleon's government had never taken physical possession of the North American territory. In New Orleans, on November 30, 1803, Spain relinquished control of Louisiana to France in a formal ceremony. French officials handed Louisiana over to the United States less than a month later, on December 20, 1803. The Louisiana Purchase was officially complete. The United States now owned the vast Louisiana territory.

THE WAR OF 1812

Thomas Jefferson wanted to purchase New Orleans and the Louisiana Territory to limit the chances that the United States might become embroiled in European conflicts. If France had exercised control over the Louisiana Territory, the United States almost certainly would have allied itself with Great Britain against France. In essence, the purchase was a means of insuring American neutrality. The continuing wars between Great Britain and France intensified throughout the first decade and a half of the nineteenth century, however. Napoleon held the upper hand in land forces, and the British relied on their superior navy. Even before Jefferson left office, in March 1809, the United States already had imposed trading and commerce restrictions on its own shipping to avoid a conflict.

Great Britain asserted the right to stop American ships to reclaim British subjects and impress them into service in the Royal Navy. Americans deplored such actions and responded with various diplomatic efforts to resolve the disputes. National pride and indignation rose over the continued abuse of American rights, however. After having exhausted peaceful options, the United States gave a decisive answer when it declared war on Great Britain in 1812.

America's aims in the War of 1812 have been a source of disagreement ever since the conflict began. The stated purpose of the war was to insure the American right to unmolested trade on the high seas. Once at war, however, the United States spent much of its time and resources waging war on British holdings in Canada and on Spanish holdings in Florida. The United States also fought against various American Indian groups, many of whom had allied themselves with Great Britain. British operatives provided the American Indians with arms and supplies. The British also made it a point to incite many tribes against the Americans, who were moving westward onto native lands in increasing numbers. Many of the Americans' efforts against American Indian tribes included the strategic goal of enabling U.S. forces to attack British Canada or the goal of preventing the British from seizing the Spanish port city of Mobile.

In short, the United States fought the War of 1812 to protect American rights, but expansionists saw the war as an opportunity. Because Great Britain held Canada and Spain held Florida, American commanders eyed the two territories as possible war trophies. The opportunity to expand American territory by waging war with Great Britain was not a sensible plan, however. The United States managed to hold its own against the British, perhaps because Great Britain was fighting another war in Europe at the time. Great Britain's ongoing war with France compelled the British to take the steps that led to the conflict with America. After the defeat and first abdication of Napoleon in 1814, Great Britain made swift moves to end the war with the United States by negotiating a peace treaty.

The Treaty of Ghent ended the War of 1812. The treaty was signed at the end of 1814 and ratified early in 1815. This treaty essentially returned things to the way they were before the war. America proclaimed its rights to free trade, and Great Britain declared its right to exercise authority over its citizens. The United States did not gain any territory in Canada and did not lose any of its western lands to Great Britain. Under the terms of the treaty, the United States returned control of Florida to Spain. The ease with which American forces had seized that colony helped to convince the Spanish government, however, that Florida would be difficult to hold. Later actions reinforced that notion.

FLORIDA

As part of the peace treaty that ended the American Revolution, the newly independent former colonies gained possession of all British lands east of the Mississippi River. In the years that followed the Revolution, the United States looked at Great Britain to the north (Canada) and Spain to the south (Florida) as potential enemies. The fledgling nation never gave the two European countries its full trust, viewing their presence in North America as a threat to American security. The War of 1812 allowed the United States to attack both British and Spanish territories. During the war, Canada remained in British hands. To the south, American forces defeated American Indian forces and exposed Florida to future encroachments. Following the war, the United States hungrily eyed Spanish Florida.

Florida posed a problem for Spain and a problem for the United States. After the Revolutionary War, Florida became a haven for escaped slaves and troublesome American Indians, who found refuge under the Spanish flag. Many of these refugees gathered at a place that became known as "Negro Fort,"

JACKSON AT PENSACOLA.

After many attacks on American Indians and frequent incursions into Spanish Florida by the U.S. Army, Spain ceded Florida to the United States. In exchange, the United States renounced any claims on all Spanish lands west of the Mississippi, in addition to $5 million. In this picture, Major General Andrew Jackson and his troops invade Pensacola, Florida, the capital of West Florida, in 1818.

from which they conducted frequent raids into American territory. Spain refused to deal with these marauders, raising the ire of U.S. citizens in nearby Georgia and Tennessee. The presence of other American Indian tribes in these regions also worried the local citizenry. One Tennessean, Andrew Jackson, decided to use his military position to alter the situation. From 1816 to 1818, Jackson forced five treaties on the Cherokee, Chickasaw, and Choctaw tribes, stripping them of land. Many Creek Indians who opposed these agreements banded together with Florida Seminole and escaped black slaves to resist the implementation of these treaties.

In early 1818, Jackson led an army south to enforce the treaty. Jackson overstepped his orders and followed the American Indians into Spanish territory. By late May, Jackson had seized Pensacola, the capital of Spanish West Florida. Jackson's actions were questionable, but he justified them by claiming that the Spanish harbored Seminole warriors in the fort at Pensacola. When Jackson captured Pensacola, he discovered no warriors there, but he maintained control of the position. Jackson's aggressive foray into Spanish territory stirred up strong responses, both for and against his actions, in the press. The administration of President James Monroe suddenly faced a public-relations predicament.

President Monroe wanted to disavow Jackson's actions and contemplated publicly condemning him. Secretary of State John Quincy Adams saw the situation as a means to a greater end, however. With American troops holding Pensacola, Adams argued that America could use this American military presence on Spanish colonial soil to force Spain to the bargaining table. Because the United States held Pensacola, American negotiators could discuss the situation from a position of strength. Adams won out, and the United States stood behind Jackson. The Americans blamed Spain for its lack of control over the Seminole, and Spain and the United States entered into negotiations.

THE ADAMS-ONÍS TREATY

Spain seemingly learned one key lesson from the War of 1812 and the First Seminole War: Spain could not defend Florida against a growing United States. Rather than suffer the indignity of losing the rest of Florida to the young nation through war, Spain came to terms with the inevitable and gave the territory away in the Adams-Onís Treaty of 1819–1821. The secretary of state (and future president) John Quincy Adams headed the negotiations for the United States. Luis de Onís represented Spain.

Following Jackson's actions, Secretary of State Adams defended the American commander. Writing to the American minister in Madrid, the Spanish capital, Adams pointed out that Spain was trying to hold on to territory that it could not defend:

> Spain must immediately make her election either to place a force in Florida adequate at once to the protection of her territory and to the fulfilment [sic] of her engagements or cede to the United States a province of which she retains nothing but the nominal possession, but which is in fact a derelict, open to the occupancy of every enemy, civilized or savage, of the United States and serving no other earthly purpose, than as a post of annoyance to them.[5]

In other words, Spain needed to invest in the defense of Florida or give the territory to the United States.

Initially, Spain was reluctant to agree to any provisions that gave both East Florida and West Florida to the United States. The treaty discussions also allowed Spain to address another concern with the United States, however: the matter of Texas. Under the terms of the Adams-Onís Treaty, the United States relinquished all claims to Texas. This ostensibly preserved the Spanish colonies in Texas from future American encroachments. Specifically, the United States recognized Spanish claims west of the Sabine River, which formed part of the boundary between Louisiana and Texas; this meant that Texas was undeniably a Spanish possession. The treaty also required the United Sates to settle U.S. citizens' claims against Spain, up to $5 million.

During the negotiations, Adams presented an entirely new condition to the Spanish. The United States wanted the western boundary of the territory under discussion, wherever it ended up being drawn, to extend all the way to the Pacific. Such a requirement solidified American claims to Oregon and raised the prospect of the United States' gaining additional western lands in the future. Before this time, American claims always had been limited by the Rocky Mountains. With this demand, the United States asserted its calling to establish itself as a transcontinental power, with claims to coastline territory on the shores of two different oceans. The Spanish negotiators were reluctant to consider this request. Adams insisted, however, and

THE LOUISIANA PURCHASE

When Napoleon Bonaparte offered to sell all of Louisiana to the United States in 1803, President Jefferson realized the enormous benefits the purchase offered to his young nation. The territory doubled the size of the United States and gave the nation room in which to grow throughout the nineteenth century. To seal the deal and work out the details, the United States and France signed three separate treaties.

In the first treaty, France disclosed the Spanish cession of Louisiana to France and turned that same territory over to the United States. Article I of the agreement included these terms:

Whereas by the Article the third of the Treaty concluded at St. Ildefonso the 9th Vendémiaire on 1st October 1800 between the First Consul of the French Republic and his Catholic Majesty it was agreed as follows.

"His Catholic Majesty promises and engages on his part to cede to the French Republic six months after the full and entire execution of the conditions and Stipulations herein relative to his Royal Highness the Duke of Parma, the Colony or Province of Louisiana with the Same extent that it now has in the hand of Spain, & that it had when eventually Spain agreed to draw a boundary line to the Pacific to protect Spanish possessions in the west. The concession served only to increase American interest in the coastal lands.

The Adams-Onís Treaty also marked the transition that was facing the Spanish empire in the Americas. Spain lost nearly all of its New World possessions in the 1810s and 1820s: Paraguay (lost in 1811); Uruguay (1815); Argentina (1816); Chile (1818);

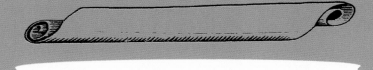

France possessed it; and Such as it Should be after the Treaties subsequently entered into between Spain and other States."

And whereas in pursuance of the Treaty and particularly of the third article the French Republic has an [incontestable] title to the domain and to the possession of the said Territory—The First Consul of the French Republic desiring to give to the United States a strong proof of his friendship doth hereby cede to the United States in the name of the French Republic for ever and in full Sovereignty the said territory with all its rights and appurtenances as fully and in the Same manner as they have been acquired by the French Republic in virtue of the above mentioned Treaty concluded with his Catholic Majesty.[*]

Because the initial treaty did not specify the exact boundaries of Louisiana, the borders were left open to future interpretation. The United States took full advantage of this vagueness, eventually claiming all of the Great Plains south of the 49th parallel.

[*] "Louisiana Purchase Treaty," The Avalon Project at Yale Law School. Available online at http://www.yale.edu/lawweb/avalon/diplomacy/france/louis1.htm.

Peru (1821); the rest of Central America (1821); and what later became the nations of Venezuela, Colombia, and Panama in 1825. In the midst of all these colonial rebellions, Mexico gained its independence from Spain in 1821. All that remained of Spain's once-vast American holdings were the island colonies of Cuba and Puerto Rico. The Adams-Onís Treaty stood to benefit the newly independent North American state of Mexico rather than the old European state of Spain. When Spain lost her colonies, the United States stood alone as the primary power in the region. Foreign policy decisions soon leveraged this reality into territorial gains for the United States.

Following the ratification of the Adams-Onís Treaty, the United States recognized Mexico, Colombia, Chile, and Argentina as independent and sovereign nations in 1822. The age of the Spanish empire in the New World was over, even as the realization of America's ideal of Manifest Destiny was beginning to emerge.

Territories and
National Policy

In the first decade of the nineteenth century, the United States greatly extended its territorial holdings through the Louisiana Purchase. Just 16 years later, the young nation added Florida to its domain, removing the threat of a foreign power from the southern portion of the continental eastern seaboard. Following the War of 1812, the United States and Great Britain often shared similar policy aims, the result being a relatively friendly and nondangerous British Canada, America's neighbor to the north. The United States soon turned its attention to the lands west of the Mississippi River. To encourage settlement in those territories, the federal government developed policies to deal with slavery and American Indians.

Despite its vast holdings of still-unsettled lands, the United States also looked beyond its borders. No longer would American influence be limited to the North American continent. American policymakers dreamed of taking on a new role in which the United States served as a force in the Western Hemisphere. The United States was coming into its own, and its domestic and foreign policies reflected the American ideal of expansion. Domestic policies also high-lighted the growing fissure between the North and South over the explosive issue of slavery. Many of these policies contrib-uted to the political climate that produced the expansionist actions of the 1840s.

THE MISSOURI COMPROMISE

In 1820, the issue of slavery and how it related to western expansion threatened to divide the young republic. The specific issue was the legal status of slavery in the western territories and future states. At the core of the controversy was whether the Missouri Territory would be admitted to the Union as a slave state or a free state. Following the admission of Alabama as a slave state, the membership of the Senate was equally divided between slave and free states. Thus, theoretically, the South could protect the institution of slavery in the Senate regardless of population growth in either the free states or the slave states.

The House and Senate fought over the matter, especially after some people suggested prohibiting slavery in all of the lands of the Louisiana Territory. An attempt to separate a por-tion of territory that belonged to Massachusetts to form the state of Maine provided the basis for a political settlement, however.

The U.S. Senate engineered a compromise. According to its terms, Missouri entered the Union as a slave state, Maine entered as a free state, and slavery was prohibited north of a parallel marked by 36°30' north latitude except for those areas north of the parallel that were included in the state of Missouri. Most of the southern border of Missouri ran along the 36°30' parallel.

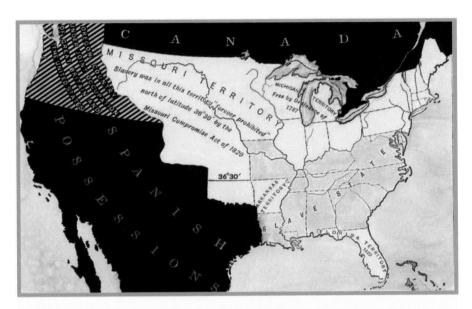

When Missouri petitioned Congress for admission to the Union, there was concern about unequal representation between the free states and the slave states. The Missouri Compromise in 1820 brought statehood for Missouri, a slave state, and Maine, a free state, and prohibited slavery in the former Louisiana Territory north of the southern boundary of Missouri.

The Missouri Compromise maintained the balance between slave states and free states in the Senate. Many people believed that the compromise laid the slavery issue to rest. As the United States acquired additional western lands, however, the issue resurfaced again, and with greater intensity. The rise of the spirit of Manifest Destiny led to territorial expansion, and that expansion, in turn, elevated the issue of slavery to greater importance. This persistent problem eventually led to the calamitous and divisive Civil War.

THE MONROE DOCTRINE

Another contributing factor to the success of America's Manifest Destiny of the 1840s was the formulation, in the 1820s, of a cornerstone of American foreign policy. That cornerstone was the Monroe Doctrine, which helped to pave the way for the acquisition of vast territories. The formulation of the Monroe Doctrine came in response to European maneuverings for territory on the North American continent. France and Russia sought British support for a move to back Spain in an attempt to recover some of the colonies that Spain had lost to revolution in the Americas. Great Britain opposed this plan, but the threat to American growth was evident.

Great Britain proposed a joint declaration with the United States to keep other European powers at bay. The British proposal included a disavowal by both the United States and Great Britain of any future acquisitions in North America. Faced with the British proposal, Secretary of State John Quincy Adams saw a rare opportunity for the United States to assert itself on the international stage. Adams opposed making a joint declaration with Great Britain. He maintained that "It would be more candid, as well as more dignified, to avow our principles explicitly to Russia and France, than to come in as a cockboat in the wake of the British man-of-war."[1] Besides, British intentions were now known and Adams wondered, "Why should the United States take part in a joint declaration by which it would gain nothing, and at the cost of a pledge not to expand?"[2] Adams also believed that colonialism was morally wrong. In Adams's view, the Monroe Doctrine offered a way to put an end to European colonization in the Americas.

President Monroe announced the new doctrine in early December 1823. It was part of the written State of the Union address that he sent to Congress each year. The so-called Monroe Doctrine included three key points. First, the United States insisted that European nations should not establish any new colonies in the Americas. Second, the United States professed continued neutrality in European affairs and wars. In agreement with his predecessors, Monroe did not intend to involve the United States in the conflicts and intrigues that often ensnared the European powers. Third, President Monroe declared that those same European states should not intervene in the affairs of independent American states, many of which had recently broken ties with Spain. Simply put, Europe was to mind the affairs of Europe, and the United States and other American nations would mind the affairs of the Americas.

The shift in policy made sense. The newly independent nations in Central and South America were vulnerable to European coercion. The Monroe Doctrine allowed the new governments to sort things out themselves—an extension of the American ideal of self-determination. Secretary of State Adams reasoned that the British government would support this American doctrine. After all, Great Britain had established economic ties with many of the former Spanish colonies. If Spain reclaimed those colonies, Great Britain would lose commercial and trade opportunities. Monroe's secretary of state was correct. Even though the United States and Great Britain did not make a joint declaration, Great Britain voiced its support for the Monroe Doctrine. The age of European colonization in the Americas was over.

THE AMERICAN POLICY OF AMERICAN INDIAN REMOVAL

Many opportunities to expand awaited the United States in the 1820s and 1830s. The young nation seemed poised to enlarge its borders. Patriotic nationalism fueled expectations of America's achieving greatness. This nationalist dream had an obvious limitation, however. Specifically, the ideals of Manifest Destiny excluded nonwhites from participating in American expansion. The forced migration of about 125,000 American Indians from the American Southeast to lands west of the Mississippi epitomized the paradox of Manifest Destiny. The nationalist dream allowed some people to fulfill their destinies while destroying the dreams of others.

The Articles of Confederation, which was the country's first constitution but formed a weak national government, empowered the federal government to deal with American Indians. So did the U.S. Constitution. Although the U.S. government did not recognize American Indian ownership of land, federal policy usually required the negotiation of treaties with tribes to advance settlement in the interior. The practice of treaty making also appeased the natives, who received some compensation for ceding land to United States. This approach was far from perfect, but it proved effective, at least for a time, "because demand for national expansion was steady but not frantic, as it would become in the ensuing decades."[3]

The growing American economy helped to increase the desire to force American Indians from the Southeast. Rising demand for cotton fueled the burning need for more land—land that the natives occupied. The American Indians who remained in the region had small landholdings, but the demand for cotton led to more encroachments upon native land. In short, "Indian relocation was driven by private greed" for American Indian lands.[4]

In the end, the federal courts determined the fate of the natives who remained in the Southeast. Unfortunately, state governments and speculators violated the American Indian rights guaranteed by the judiciary. In 1832, the state of Georgia lost a key court battle in *Worcester v. Georgia.* In that case, the U.S. Supreme Court ruled against the state's policy of American Indian removal. Chief Justice John Marshall, writing for the majority, declared Georgia's American Indian relocation laws unconstitutional. Georgia defied the ruling, however, and President Andrew Jackson supposedly said, "Well, John Marshall has made his decision: *now let him enforce it!*"[5] Whether Jackson made the remark is questionable, but his administration's policy of noninterference in state attempts to relocate natives demonstrates Jackson's desire to remove American Indians and send them westward.

The policy of relocation continued. In 1831–1838, this policy resulted in the migration that has come to be known as the Trail of Tears and the establishment of Indian Territory in what

After Andrew Jackson passed the Indian Removal Act in 1830, a year later nearly 15,000 Choctaw Indians were forced to relocate from their homelands in the American South to present-day Oklahoma. Many suffered from exposure, disease, and starvation along the way. The route they traveled is now known as the Trail of Tears, shown in the painting above. The removal of the Seminole (1832), the Creek (1834), the Chickasaw (1837), and the Cherokee (1838) soon followed.

is now Oklahoma. American cravings for desirable land continued to grow. For the unfortunate Cherokee and other tribes who were forced to relocate west of the Mississippi, the relocation stalled the eventual seizure of more land only temporarily.

LAND POLICY UNDER THE ARTICLES OF CONFEDERATION

From the time of its founding, the United States of America sought to expand westward. This is evident in federal land policy, even under the Articles of Confederation. Throughout its brief existence in the 1780s, the Confederation Congress suffered from a lack of funds. The young nation enjoyed a surplus of western lands, however. Various states laid claim to portions of these lands. Most of the claims dated back to original colonial charters. The charters often conflicted with one another, however, and granted the same land rights to different parties. The Confederation government sought to tackle these issues and generate revenue at the same time.

THE ORDINANCE OF 1785

In 1785, the Confederation Congress enacted a land ordinance that served as the basis for American land policy for nearly 80 years. The U.S. government lacked authority to generate revenue through taxation. Under the Land Ordinance of 1785, the U.S. government surveyed western lands to sell them. The federal government divided these lands into townships, each one six miles by six miles in size. Each township was divided further into sections of 640 acres, or parcels of one square mile. Speculators purchased the 640-acre sections and subdivided them into smaller tracts to resell to settlers.

A significant feature of this land ordinance was the emphasis that it placed on public education. The government reserved the sixteenth section of each township for the express purpose of funding public schools. Local communities could sell the land to fund a local school or build the school on the section, which was centrally located within the township. The long-term effects of this single legislative act are still evident across the United States today. The importance of the 1785 Land Ordinance was far-reaching. The Confederation Congress passed another land act two years later, however, the implications of which had an even greater impact on the young nation.

THE NORTHWEST ORDINANCE OF 1787

The Confederation Congress faced several challenges in 1787. The young government lacked money, which resulted in the sale of western lands. Because several states held competing claims to many of these western lands, as settlers moved west and began to populate these disputed areas, questions of jurisdiction arose. Finally, although slavery was confined mostly to the South, the question of slavery arose in discussions of territories north and west of the original 13 colonies.

To resolve these issues, in 1787, the Confederation Congress passed the Northwest Ordinance. This law forced all states to cede their claims to western lands to the federal government. The law also established the precedent whereby the national government, not the states, directed the affairs of the territories. Thus, as the eighteenth century gave way to the nineteenth, and the United States expanded its holdings as part of its Manifest Destiny, the question of slavery in territory acquired in the 1840s served as the central political issue in the 1850s.

The Northwest Ordinance created the model by which future western lands became official U.S. territories and then states. Congress organized a region into a territory and appointed a territorial governor and other officials. Later legislative acts allowed the president to appoint the governor, with Senate approval. After it reached a population of 5,000 people, a territory could organize a territorial legislature. A territory needed a minimum population of 60,000 people to apply for statehood. In 1803, Ohio became the first state from the Northwest Territory to enter the Union. Eventually, the remaining Northwest Territory yielded four other states: Indiana, Illinois, Michigan, and Wisconsin. All five of these entered the Union as free states.

The Northwest Ordinance prohibited slavery in the Northwest Territory. The ordinance stated, "There shall be neither slavery nor involuntary servitude in the said territory, otherwise than in the punishment of crime . . ."[6] This provision is curious, because some northern states still allowed slavery at the time the ordinance was enacted. Despite this apparent inconsistency, the ordinance banned slavery from this large section of territory intended for future states.

One practical implication of the Northwest Ordinance was the bringing into existence of adjoining northern states, all of which prohibited slavery. These free states participated in and influenced the national debate on Manifest Destiny and slavery during the 1840s and 1850s. In 1820, the Missouri Compromise essentially extended free territory west of the Mississippi River across the northern Great Plains to the Rockies.

JOHN QUINCY ADAMS
(1767–1848)

Architect of American Destiny

John Quincy Adams was one of the key players who fashioned American foreign policy in the 1810s and 1820s. As secretary of state, he led the way by negotiating the Adams-Onís Treaty and designing the Monroe Doctrine, a series of principles that set the course for American foreign policy for the next century. So what else do historians know about this influential man?

John Quincy Adams was the son of John and Abigail Adams. He was born on July 11, 1767, in Braintree, Massachusetts. As a boy, John Quincy Adams traveled to Europe with his father, who served as an American diplomat and representative to various countries. The younger Adams graduated from Harvard and practiced law before following in his father's footsteps and entering diplomatic service. John Quincy Adams represented his country in the Netherlands, the German states, and Russia. The younger Adams also served a term in the U.S. Senate. In 1817, President James Monroe appointed

LAND POLICY IN THE U.S. CONSTITUTION

The U.S. Constitution allowed for western growth in at least one significant way, under Congressional powers. Specifically, the Constitution empowered Congress "to dispose of and make all needful Rules and Regulations respecting the Territory or other Property belonging to the United States."[7] Congress therefore could establish the path to eventual statehood for territories. The Founders apparently viewed the American West as land that ultimately would become part of the United States. The American Constitution was unique because it provided for

John Quincy Adams as secretary of state, a role in which Adams excelled.

Although he lost the popular vote, John Quincy Adams won the controversial election of 1824 and became the first son of a president to win the presidency. Despite the lack of support, Adams still pursued his domestic agenda aggressively. He sought to link the nation together through a system of canals and highways. After Adams lost his bid for reelection in 1828, he won election to the House of Representatives in 1830. As a member of Congress, Adams won the repeal of the so-called "gag rule" that prohibited antislavery resolutions from advancing out of House committees. In 1841, Adams successfully took part in a case before the U.S. Supreme Court in which he defended a group of captured Africans that revolted against their captors aboard the *Amistad*. On February 21, 1848, Adams was at his seat in the House chamber when he suffered a stroke. The great American statesman and architect of American destiny died two days later.

lands as yet unclaimed to become territories and then states. The Constitution promised equal representation and full rights as U.S. citizens to the residents of these new states. In other words, the Constitution allowed future states to help rule the federal government.

Oregon

The Lewis and Clark expedition of 1804–1806 proved that no waterway connected the east and west coasts of North America. The expedition brought back descriptions of flora, fauna, and native peoples in the territories they explored, however. One of these territories was Oregon.

Soon after the return of Lewis and Clark, enterprising settlers began to migrate westward, over the vast expanse now known as the Great Plains. Americans in the early nineteenth century, however, viewed the region as the Great American Desert. American explorer Zebulon Pike journeyed through the region from 1806 to 1807. Pike's report incorrectly labeled the land as "wholly unfit for cultivation."[1] Farther west, however, beyond the Rocky Mountains and along the Pacific Coast, lay Oregon, a rich land that held much promise for Americans. The Oregon Country was immense. It included the territory between the Pacific Ocean and the Rockies and stretched southward to the northern border of Mexico.

The United States was one of four nations that laid claim to the Oregon Territory. The other three—Spain, Russia, and Great Britain—established their claims long before the United States. This did not deter the young nation from maintaining its own right to this land, however.

SPANISH CLAIMS

Spanish claims to Oregon predated those of any other colonial power. Spain's claim dated back to 1494, just two years after Christopher Columbus's historic first voyage. To avoid a conflict between Portugal and Spain, Pope Alexander VI negotiated a treaty between the two Catholic seafaring powers. The Treaty of Tordesillas recognized Spain as the authority over all of North America, including Oregon.

After England broke its ties with the Roman Catholic Church in the early sixteenth century, the now-Protestant nation of Great Britain no longer recognized the Spanish claims. Russia, which did not accept papal authority, also disputed the notion of Spanish rights in the region. Because the United States was not yet independent or even settled at the time that these claims were first made, it was a latecomer to the exploration of, settlement in, and diplomatic wrangling about Oregon.

Following the Treaty of Tordesillas, Spain explored the region and continued to assert its claim to the western coast. The Spanish never established themselves as a strong presence in the territory, however. They maintained that they owned Oregon, but they never really took possession of their claims. As a result, as Spain's position as a world power declined during the latter decades of the eighteenth century, Spain's claims to Oregon became less believable. Spain's great rival, Great Britain, was one of the powers that threatened Spain's hold on Oregon.

The Spanish and English nearly came to war over portions of the Pacific Northwest, a region both claimed for hundreds of years. In a series of three agreements called the Nootka Conventions, war was averted and the Spanish monopoly ended along the Pacific Coast. Pictured is a depiction of Captain James Cook of the British Royal Navy, one of the first Europeans to set foot on British Columbian soil, when he visited what is now known as Friendly Cove on Nootka Island.

Great Britain traced its claims to Oregon to 1579, when Sir Francis Drake claimed the area during the famous voyage in which he circumnavigated the globe. In 1778, in the early stages of his last voyage, Captain James Cook landed at Nootka Sound, on what today is Vancouver Island in British Columbia, Canada. Cook claimed the area for Great Britain. Ten years later, British merchant John Meares established an outpost on Nootka Sound to trade furs with China. The presence of Meares and his British crews disturbed the Spanish authorities.

In 1789, Spain decided to act against British and Russian encroachment. Spanish forces established firm control over Nootka Island and confiscated the property of John Meares. Because of the incident, the possibility of war loomed. Great Britain and Spain wanted to avoid a conflict, however. In the 1790s, they negotiated a series of agreements known as the Nootka Convention. Rather than fight over Oregon, the two powers agreed to allow each other to trade at Nootka Sound. The agreements did not settle the question of ownership, however, and precise boundaries were not determined. Instead, the convention essentially allowed anyone to settle and trade in the area. Thus, Great Britain could legally establish settlements and carry on commercial trade in Oregon while the question of ownership remained unanswered. The Nootka Convention also opened the door for the United States to enter later as a competitor for ownership. Under the Adams-Onís Treaty of 1819, Spain recognized American rights north of the 42nd parallel, including Oregon.

Spain concentrated its resources in ultimately failed attempts to hold on to its other American possessions. By 1825, however, revolutions had driven Spain from the North American mainland. The newly independent nation of Mexico inherited all Spanish claims to the Oregon Country, including those recognized in the Adams-Onís Treaty.

RUSSIAN CLAIMS

Russia also laid claim to the Oregon country. In 1741, Danish-born Vitus Bering sailed for the Russian czar and explored the Pacific coast of North America. The water that separates northern Asia from North America bears his name: the Bering Strait. Initially, the Russians contented themselves with the lucrative fur trade conducted through outposts in the Aleutian Islands. In 1799, however, the founding of the Russian-American Company signified the Russians' intended expansion southward. In 1821, Russia's czar Alexander I asserted Russian ownership of all lands north of the 51st parallel, slightly north of Vancouver Island.

The move provoked a strong response from the United States. American secretary of state John Quincy Adams voiced strong disapproval of the Russian claim. So did the government of Great Britain. The strength of the British navy forced Russia to negotiate the situation. In 1824, the United States concluded an agreement under which Russia renounced all claims south of 54°40' north latitude. A year later, under the terms of the Anglo-Russian Treaty, Russia gave up its remaining claims to land within Oregon. The United States and Great Britain now were the only nations with the potential to inherit the large Oregon Country.

BRITISH CLAIMS

Great Britain first laid claim to parts of Oregon in 1579, when Sir Francis Drake landed north of San Francisco Bay. The explorer claimed the land for Queen Elizabeth, but he was far more interested in engaging Spanish galleons than in founding a settlement. For two centuries, the British did nothing else in the region. They returned in 1778, when Captain James Cook landed on Vancouver Island. Like Drake before him, Cook claimed the land and then left. This time, however, someone else, British trader John Meares, followed him.

The Nootka Convention averted a costly fight over Oregon. More importantly, the agreements did not determine who held the rights to Oregon. Consequently, neither Great Britain nor Spain acted as the dominant force in Oregon. This lack of clarity later allowed the fledgling United States to assert its own claims to Oregon.

CLAIMS BY THE UNITED STATES

The United States was the last nation to lay claim to Oregon. Americans could not contend that their people were the first to explore or settle the area. After all, Spanish, Russian, and British claims predated the adoption of the U.S. Constitution. The original Louisiana Purchase, which did not clearly define the extent of the Louisiana Territory, was virtually the only basis for an American claim to Oregon. This was not a firm negotiation point, as France had taken the imprecisely drawn territory from Spain and sold it, still undefined, to the United States. Although Spain maintained some claims to the region, it was mostly British and American merchants who were vying for primacy in Oregon. The two sides wanted the same patch of land on the south bank of the Columbia River.

Other border disagreements threatened to grow into larger issues. The situation nearly spun out of control in 1817. Many Americans did not trust Great Britain, and the British presence in Canada was unsettling. British public opinion allowed the British cabinet to sign away rights in North America, if necessary, to keep the peace. In the meantime, both the United States and Great Britain faced the prospect of having a hostile neighbor and unsettled border. The necessity of conducting traffic on the Great Lakes provided the perfect opportunity for either or both nations to assert themselves. To avoid a costly and dangerous escalation of naval ships on the Great Lakes, Great Britain and the United States demilitarized the lakes. The resulting harmony between the two nations endures to this day, as does one of the longest and most peaceful boundaries in the world. In 1818, the two nations continued to talk of ways to work out territorial disputes. The only remaining territory in question was Oregon.

POSTPONING THE OREGON QUESTION

Ownership of Oregon was something that both the American and British governments claimed, yet neither nation seemed willing to go to war over it. Lord Castlereagh, Great Britain's foreign secretary from 1812 to 1822, did not want his country to lose face over the Oregon question. Castlereagh recognized, however, that American ownership of Oregon did not necessarily threaten British interests in the region. Even so, Castlereagh did not intend to cede the issue—or the territory—to the United States. Castlereagh insisted that even though Great Britain was returning Fort Astoria, a fur-trading center on the south shore of the Columbia River, to American control in 1818, the move did not mean that Great Britain was withdrawing any of its claims to territory south of the Columbia River. Unfortunately, British envoys never communicated Lord Castlereagh's message to the U.S. government. Instead, American officials saw only the British act of withdrawing their operations north of the Columbia River. Understandably, the United States now believed that Great Britain had no aims to assert ownership over territory south of the Columbia River.

During the next decade, Spain (in 1819) and Russia (in 1824–1825) both signed agreements in which they gave up their claims to territory in Oregon. In 1823, in the Monroe Doctrine, the United States maintained that the Americas, North and South, were off-limits to any additional European colonization. At the very least, this 10-year postponement reduced the number of claimants at the negotiating table.

Initially, having fewer claimants did not result in lower tensions. Great Britain believed that the Columbia River should be the border, after the example of the St. Lawrence River, which partially served as a boundary between the United States and British Canada in the east. The Hudson's Bay Company favored this approach and recommended setting the 49th parallel as the border until that parallel intersected the Columbia. From that point, the Columbia would serve as the border until the river reached the Pacific Ocean. The American government rebuffed such offers, and the question remained unresolved. After 10 years of negotiations, each side still disputed the other side's claims. All negotiations stalled, and in 1828, the two sides could agree only to extend the original agreement indefinitely. Either the United States or Great Britain could reopen the issue by giving the other side a one-year notice to terminate the agreement. Thus, the question of Oregon ownership remained unanswered for nearly 20 years.

THE OREGON TRAIL

The difficulty in getting to Oregon impeded the settlement of the territory. Few people knew the way across the continent, although various expeditions revealed parts of a workable route. One of these expeditions discovered the South Pass, which offered an easier way through the Rocky Mountains. Trappers and backwoods traders trapped, hunted, and traveled in the mountains and plains, learning the geography. These so-called mountain men learned the way west, and many of them offered their services as guides across the plains, through the mountains to Oregon. Much of this knowledge was unknown to the rest of American society, however. In the 1830s, published accounts of Oregon and descriptions of the overland route motivated many Americans to head west. In 1843, a wagon train of more than a thousand pioneers left Independence, Missouri, for Oregon.

As more Americans learned of the overland route, more settlers made their way to Oregon. The 2,000-mile trek was far from easy, however. These sojourners faced disease, severe weather, and many dangers. Many pioneers died along the way. Despite the challenges, each spring scores of eager settlers set out on the trail to Oregon. On their arrival in Oregon, most of these settlers settled south of the Columbia River. By 1846, about 5,000 Americans had arrived in the territory and settled south of the Columbia.

The British could not ignore such numbers. Nor could the Hudson's Bay Company hope to reestablish itself south of the

The Oregon Trail, which spanned over half of North America through land later to be known as Missouri, Kansas, Nebraska, Wyoming, Idaho, Oregon, and Washington, expanded the nation from the Atlantic to the Pacific. The trail was first used by missionaries, fur traders, and the military. In 1843, an estimated thousand emigrants (followed by hundreds of thousands more) traveled the trail to claim land in the West.

Columbia. The increasing numbers of people in the area meant more competition for furs. Then, in 1843, the American settlers formed their own provisional government. Rather than fight a losing battle, in 1845, the Hudson's Bay Company moved the center of its operations north to Vancouver Island. At about the same time, despite their claims, the British virtually abandoned their presence south of the Columbia. By the mid-1840s, the Hudson's Bay Company and American settlers seemed to have

worked things out for themselves. Their respective governments needed a little more time to agree to any agreement
concerning Oregon, however.

FINAL RESOLUTION OF THE OREGON QUESTION

The relocation of the Hudson's Bay Company to Vancouver
Island should have ended much of the boundary dispute
between Great Britain and the United States. Despite the move,
however, Great Britain insisted on making the Columbia River
the boundary. The United States, gripped by the ideals of Manifest Destiny, responded by increasing its traditional demand for
a border at the 49th parallel to include the entire coastline to 54°
40' north latitude. This parallel represented the southern boundary of Russian territory. Such a claim amounted to a demand to
expel Great Britain from the western coast altogether. Both sides
repeatedly stated their unyielding demands, and negotiations
stalled. In the United States, the presidential election campaign
of 1844 included strong words about Oregon. Democratic
candidate James K. Polk offered the slogan "Fifty-four forty or
fight" as shorthand for a solution to the Oregon question. Many
Americans apparently agreed; they voted Polk into office.

Following the election, Great Britain attempted to sidestep
the issue by proposing that a third party act as an arbiter to
settle the dispute. Outgoing President John Tyler turned down
the proposal. On March 4, 1845, Polk took the oath of office
as president. In his inaugural address, he assured Americans
that he intended "to assert and maintain by all constitutional
means the right of the United States to that portion of our
territory which lies beyond the Rocky Mountains."[2] Polk also
maintained that American claims to the Oregon Country were
"clear and unquestionable."[3] The new president even voiced
support for offering Oregon residents the full protection of
American law. Despite this show of bravado, both sides desired
a peaceful resolution to the issue. Tensions and fears rose over
the heightened rhetoric, however.

President Polk now faced the prospect of having to back down from his "Fifty-four forty or fight" campaign promise. The president looked for a way to salvage the existing treaty without causing too much political pain. Polk found a way out that involved two steps. First, he produced three proposals from previous administrations in which the United States offered to draw the boundary at the 49th parallel. Secretary of State James Buchanan made the offer to Great Britain just four months into Polk's term of office, on July 12, 1845. The British minister to the United States immediately rejected the offer. This demonstrated how badly eroded relations between the two nations had become. In response, Polk withdrew the offer and demanded the line of 54°40'. Under the terms of the 1827 agreement, he also asked Congress to authorize giving Great Britain a one-year notice that the United States would no longer abide by that agreement. Congress passed the bill authorizing the notice on April 27, 1846.

For his second step, Polk found some protection in the U.S. Constitution, which directs the president to seek the "advice and consent" of the Senate.[4] All previous treaties had undergone the necessary "consent" portion of the constitutional requirements, which required a supermajority of two-thirds to approve the treaty for ratification. Only America's first president, George Washington, had ever offered a treaty to the Senate for its "advice," however. Washington's exercise had ended in frustration as the Senate offered little advice and seemingly no productive counsel on the matter. Until Polk, no president after Washington had bothered to ask the Senate what it thought about a treaty before asking the Senate to approve it.

Polk decided to ask for the Senate's advice on a measure that reiterated the claims to a border at the 49th parallel that Polk saw in the existing treaty. The ploy worked. The senators argued and wrangled over the agreement, and many of them reached the same conclusion as Polk: The 1827 treaty already granted the United States all of its traditional claims in the

OPENING OREGON FOR ALL: THE NOOTKA CONVENTION

Great Britain and Spain signed the first of several agreements known as the Nootka Convention on October 28, 1790. The agreements ended Spanish settlement and Pacific trade claims that dated to the 1494 Treaty of Tordesillas. Before the 1790 accords, the Spanish had claimed all of the Pacific Northwest, creating friction with the British. Great Britain was a stronger power than Spain and forced a pact on its declining rival. Under the agreement, both countries recognized the right of the other to establish settlements on unoccupied territory. Each nation faced no limitations on sailing, fishing, or trading in the Pacific Ocean.

The Nootka Convention created a power vacuum in Oregon. As more and more Americans poured into the territory, the United States managed to establish itself as one of the contenders for ownership of Oregon. When Spain lost its New World possessions, the United States negotiated a similar agreement with Great Britain. Eventually the presence of so many American citizens in Oregon made it virtually impossible for the British to expel the settlers. The United States now held the advantage and managed to force a favorable pact on the British. Here is the text from the original Nootka Convention, Article III:

> And in order to strengthen the bonds of friendship and to preserve in the future a perfect harmony and good understanding between the two contracting parties, it is agreed that their respective subjects shall not be disturbed or molested either in navigating or carrying on their fisheries in the Pacific Ocean or in the South Seas, or in landing on the coasts of those seas in places not already occupied, for the purpose of carrying on their commerce with the natives of the country or of making establishments there.[*]

---

[*] *Ethelbert O.S. Scholefield*, British Columbia From Earliest Times to the Present *(Vancouver, B.C.: S.J. Clarke, 1914), p. 664.*

Pacific Northwest, the 1844 campaign pledge of "Fifty-four forty or fight" notwithstanding. Moreover, no new treaty was likely to include better terms for the United States.

The Senate debated the treaty for two days before ratifying it on June 18, 1846. Those who favored claiming all of Oregon at any cost—even war with Great Britain—lacked the necessary votes to block Senate approval. Critics condemned the measure and the president, but the ratified treaty ended the threat of a war with Great Britain at the very moment the United States was at war with Mexico. In short, political realities had changed. The United States needed to avoid fighting two wars at once, especially if one of those wars was with Great Britain, the world's naval superpower. The Senate recognized this and voted to approve the treaty.

Under the terms of the treaty, the 49th parallel became the boundary between the United States and British Canada. The agreement also protected free navigation of all rivers that crossed the boundary, including the Columbia River. The Oregon question was finally resolved. For Polk and for the United States, the war with Mexico now demanded full attention.

Texas

Oregon certainly played its role in the fulfillment of Manifest Destiny. It was in Texas, however, that the best and worst of Manifest Destiny exposed itself, revealing the dual nature of American expansion. The nation that was founded on the principles of freedom and self-determination found itself waging a war to protect the borders of a slave state. The conflict began when American citizens moved to Texas and, once there, insisted on retaining American rights. The inevitable clash with Mexico led to an independent Texas that sought to enter a sympathetic Union.

THE REPUBLIC OF TEXAS

Spain governed Texas from 1690 until 1821, when Mexico (New Spain) gained its independence. During that time, Spain oversaw the so-called Kingdom of Texas as a distinct colony.

The United States conceded all claims to Texas in the Adams-Onís Treaty of 1819. The ink was barely dry on the American signatures on that treaty, however, when large numbers of Americans began moving to Texas. After breaking from Spain in 1821, Mexico claimed ownership of Texas.

The newly formed Mexican government wanted to populate Texas but found it nearly impossible to persuade Mexicans to settle there. Wanting to develop the territory, Mexico encouraged Americans to move to Texas. The Mexican government gave a land grant first to an American named Moses Austin and then, after the father's death, to Austin's son Stephen. Stephen Austin recruited 300 families to settle in Texas. Although a change in Mexican leadership disrupted these plans, Austin eventually secured a land grant and additional agreements that allowed him to recruit another 900 families to settle in Texas. Austin and these so-called Texians brought slavery into the territory. Before long, many other Americans poured into Texas. Despite Austin's agreements with Mexico, which guaranteed the primacy of Catholicism in Texas, most American settlers brought their Protestant beliefs and practices with them. By 1830, these efforts to populate Texas had resulted in about 20,000 American settlers living in Texas. These immigrants far outnumbered the local Mexican population. The government of Mexico began to try to inhibit immigration by banning the importation of slaves and hinting that slavery might be banned altogether.

In 1835, the political climate changed dramatically for the Texians. The president of Mexico, Antonio López de Santa Anna, sought to consolidate federal power and invalidated Mexico's 1824 constitution. Santa Anna recognized that the Texians, with their Protestant religion and English language, posed a threat to the sovereignty of the Mexican nation. Mexico had abolished slavery, but Americans living within Texas ignored the regulation. Many of these same American citizens objected to the increased level of interference by the Mexican

In this mural, Stephen F. Austin, the "Father of Texas" (in black over-coat), and Baron de Bastrop (seated), land commissioner of Mexico, issue land to the colonists in 1823 on the Colorado River, not far from present-day Bay City, Texas.

government. Many of these objections grew into appeals to the American government for protection from the ever-increasing interventions of the Mexican government. The situation worsened until the Texians initiated the Texas Revolution. The settlers followed the American example of 1776 and declared their independence from Mexico in 1836. The fight for the independence of Texas had begun.

During the Texas Revolution, the Texians, now called Texans, suffered setbacks at first. Among these was the loss, in March 1836, of the Battle of the Alamo. The Texans recovered, regrouped, and won an astounding victory against the Mexican forces in April 1836 at the Battle of San Jacinto. The victorious Texans forced a settlement that guaranteed them their independence from Mexico. The Mexican government later rejected the treaties signed after the battle and continued to claim Texas as a Mexican territory. By the terms of the treaties, however, and according to a newly ratified constitution, the Republic of Texas was born in 1836. The fledgling republic sought to enter the Union as a new state. The politics of slavery prevented this from happening until 1845, however. Northern opposition to the addition of another slave state meant that Texas had to wait until the political climate changed.

The fact that Texas wanted to join the United States was predictable. A few years before the Texas Revolution, French visitor Alexis de Tocqueville traveled through America and recorded many of his observations. He correctly predicted that Texas, although under Mexican control, soon would belong to the United States. De Tocqueville wrote:

> The lands of the New World belong to the first occupant; and they are the natural reward of the swiftest pioneer. Even the countries which are already peopled will have some difficulty in securing themselves from this invasion. I have already alluded to what is taking place in the province of Texas. The inhabitants of the United States are perpetually migrating to Texas, where they purchase land; and although they conform to the laws of the country, they are gradually founding the empire of their own language and their own manners. The province of Texas is still part of the Mexican dominions, but it will soon contain no Mexicans; the same thing has occurred whenever the Anglo-Americans have come into contact with populations of a different origin.[1]

As de Tocqueville correctly foresaw, the migration of Americans into Texas virtually insured that Texas became more American than Mexican. The result was the assimilation of Texas into the United States rather than the assimilation of Americans into Mexico.

JOHN TYLER

In 1844, President John Tyler found himself in a difficult political situation. To explain that difficulty requires a bit of background information.

In April 1841, on the death of President William Henry Harrison, John Tyler became the first vice president to assume the presidency. There was some confusion as to whether the Constitution allowed the vice president to become president or simply allowed him to serve in place of the president. After Harrison died of pneumonia, Tyler took the oath of office on the advice of the president's cabinet. This ended the debate as to how the system worked when a president died in office. Tyler then gave an inaugural address, thereby reinforcing his new status as president of the United States. Until 1967, Tyler's example served as the precedent in similar situations. In that year, more than 125 years later, the necessary number of states ratified the 25th Amendment to the Constitution, which spelled out presidential succession.

Tyler's political career was anything but typical. Born in 1790, he was the son of a future governor of Virginia. He also was the first American president born after the Revolutionary War and the adoption of the Constitution. After Tyler graduated from the College of William and Mary, he studied law with his father. He served as a member of the Virginia House of Delegates from 1811 to 1816. In that year, he won election to the U.S. Congress to fill a vacancy. He was reelected in 1818, but poor health forced him not to seek another term. In 1813, Tyler also volunteered and won appointment as a captain in Virginia's state militia. In 1823, he returned to the Virginia House of Delegates. He served as governor of Virginia from 1825 to 1827. During all this time in public service, Tyler gained national recognition for his opposition to increasing the power and influence of the federal government. He was a supporter of states' rights. Notably, he openly voiced his disapproval of the 1820 Missouri Compromise.

After he left the governor's office, Tyler served at the Virginia State Constitutional Convention in 1828 and 1829. He had already turned his attention once again to national politics. He won election to the U.S. Senate in 1827 as a Democratic Republican. The party was in the process of breaking apart. Tyler initially aligned himself with the Democratic wing of the party and was a supporter of President Andrew Jackson. He soon fell out with Jackson, however. The disagreement took place during the Nullification Crisis of 1832. This crisis occurred when South Carolina attempted to make null and void a national tariff policy that had been enacted after the War of 1812 to promote American manufacturing over British competition.

Tyler won reelection to the Senate in 1833, but he resigned his seat in 1836 rather than vote to expunge (reverse) the Senate's 1834 censure of Jackson for withdrawing U.S. funds from the Bank of the United States in 1833, thereby causing the bank to close. In 1839, Tyler served as a delegate in the Virginia State House.

In 1840, Tyler joined the Whig Party. He promptly won the vice presidential nomination as running mate to William Henry Harrison, a war hero. Harrison had won fame for his victory at the Battle of Tippecanoe in the War of 1812. The two men made a strong political ticket, and their campaign slogan of "Tippecanoe and Tyler, too" became one of the most memorable in presidential election history. The Whig ticket defeated the incumbent Democratic president, Martin Van Buren. Harrison's inauguration was held on March 4, 1841. He fell ill and died a month later. His death ushered in a tumultuous presidency, that of John Tyler, that revealed deep sectional fissures within the United States.

THE TYLER PRESIDENCY

As president, John Tyler quickly returned to his roots as an advocate of states' rights. The former Democrat was elected to the vice presidency as a Whig, but as president he governed more as a Democrat than as a Whig. The new president vetoed nearly every bill on the Whigs' legislative agenda, including two vetoes of Senate stalwart Henry Clay's bill to establish a national bank. The Whigs retaliated by revoking Tyler's party membership during the first year of his presidency. Every member of his cabinet—except for Secretary of State Daniel Webster, who was out of the country negotiating a treaty—resigned in September 1841. Webster left the administration in May 1842. Critics described Tyler as the man without a party.

Tyler continued to fight with the Whig-controlled Congress. In 1843, following his veto of a tariff bill, the U.S. House of Representatives contemplated impeaching the president. This was the first impeachment resolution ever introduced into or considered by the House. John Quincy Adams, a former president and member of Congress, chaired a committee that concluded that President Tyler had misused his power to veto. The House considered the impeachment resolution, but the measure failed to pass. Throughout his term in office, Tyler worked more closely with the Democrats than with the party that elected him. Practically speaking, a Democrat served for all but one month of the first Whig presidency.

Tyler's appointment of John C. Calhoun as secretary of state in 1844 marked a turning point in his presidency. Although the South Carolinian served for only a year in that post, his presence helped to define the sectional alignment of the two political parties. Increasingly, the force of the Whig Party became concentrated in the North. At the same time, the Democrats strengthened their hold on the South. The Tyler presidency exposed the seeds of the tumultuous divide of the 1850s. John Tyler served out the remainder of his term rejected by the Whigs and not trusted by the Democrats. When the time came to select candidates for the 1844 presidential election, both parties ignored the incumbent president. Whigs and Democrats alike snubbed Tyler in favor of other nominees.

A PIVOTAL ELECTION

The Democrats entered their nominating convention a divided party. A former Democratic president, Martin Van Buren, was the favorite to win the nomination. A slight majority of the delegates supported Van Buren. The convention rules required a two-thirds majority to win the nomination, however. The former president publicly opposed the immediate annexation of Texas, which placed him at odds with a large number of the delegates. Van Buren failed to win the necessary votes on the first ballot, and his support declined on each subsequent vote. The former president's support evaporated as his backers became convinced that the convention would never nominate him. On the eighth ballot, someone nominated James K. Polk, a relative unknown, for consideration. Momentum shifted toward Polk, and he won the necessary two-thirds vote on the ninth ballot. Polk became the first "dark horse" candidate for president. A dark-horse candidate is an individual who was not seen as a likely contender before the convention.

Following Polk's nomination, the Democrats selected Silas Wright, a senator from New York, as the vice presidential candidate. A strong supporter of Van Buren, Wright refused to accept the nomination. The delegates then named another senator, George Mifflin Dallas, to the ticket. Dallas agreed to run with Polk.

Polk reacted stoically when he learned of his nomination, responding with these words: "It has been well observed that the office of President of the United States should neither be sought nor declined. I have never sought it, nor should I feel at liberty to decline it, if conferred upon me by the voluntary suffrages of my fellow citizens."[2]

Predictably, the Whigs nominated Henry Clay, one of their party leaders. Clay had lost the presidential elections of 1824 and 1832, but he was one of the most recognizable figures in America. His nomination conveyed the Whigs' commitment to the issues of the previous two decades. In many respects,

James K. Polk was the eleventh president of the United States (1845–1849). He was committed to geographic expansion and was responsible for the second-largest expansion of the nation, first by securing the Oregon Territory (Washington, Oregon, and Idaho), a total of about 285,000 square miles. He then acquired 525,000 square miles through the Treaty of Guadalupe Hidalgo. The treaty reignited the debate over expanding slavery in the new territories.

Clay was a candidate of the past who was facing a candidate of the future. Polk's vision of the future promised to expand the territorial holdings of the United States. A Clay presidency promised to resurrect a national bank and extend the political maneuverings of the 1830s well into the 1840s.

Polk proved to be a capable campaigner. He realized that the issue of Texas allowed the Whigs to accuse him of being proslavery. To counter this, Polk coupled the issue of Texas annexation with an unequivocal demand that the United States obtain all of the Oregon Territory. With his "Fifty-four forty or fight!" campaign slogan, he promised to settle the Oregon and Texas questions once and for all. During the course of the campaign, Polk's message resonated with the electorate. Clay eventually offered limited support for adding Texas to the United States while ruling out war as a means of annexation. Thus, the campaign of 1844 centered on the ideals of nationalism and the question of western expansion.

The electorate chose the leadership and vision of a growing America offered by James K. Polk over the tired ideas presented by Henry Clay. Polk barely won the popular vote, but he easily defeated Clay in the electoral college. Polk's election pointed the way to American expansion and the settlement of the North American continent.

Outgoing president John Tyler learned of the election results and pondered how to conduct himself in the final months of his presidency. Texas was a self-proclaimed and independent republic. The United States and Texas negotiated a treaty in which Texas entered the Union. Tyler pushed for the annexation of Texas, but he lacked the two-thirds vote in the Senate that was required to approve a treaty. Believing that the election validated Polk's expansionist convictions, Tyler engineered the annexation of Texas by a joint resolution of Congress on March 1, 1845—three days before Polk took office.

Although Texas entered the Union while Tyler was president, the details of how the annexation issue would be resolved were left to the Polk administration. Mexico rejected the annexation of Texas, insisting on their rights to the territory. President Polk soon addressed the matter with Mexico. He did so through diplomatic channels and by making use of the U.S. military.

ANTONIO LÓPEZ DE SANTA ANNA
(1794–1876)

The Rogue of Texas History

No history of Texas is complete without the story of its chief enemy, Santa Anna. Antonio López de Santa Anna was born in 1794 in the city of Veracruz, Mexico. Initially trained by the Spanish, Santa Anna rose through the ranks of the army and eventually fought for Mexican independence from Spain. He first ascended to power when he won the Mexican presidency in 1833. During the next 22 years, Santa Anna ruled Mexico no fewer than 11 different times.

Santa Anna was a key player in three significant series of episodes involving Mexico, Texas, and the United States. In each of these series of events, Mexico gave up territory and Santa Anna lost power or status. The first events occurred during the Texas Revolution. After Santa Anna defeated the Texians (later Texans) at the battles of the Alamo and Goliad, in 1836 during the early stages of the Texas Revolution, his self-assurance grew. His overconfidence led to his overwhelming defeat and capture at the Battle of San Jacinto. Santa Anna's captors forced him to sign a treaty recognizing Texan independence. Although the Mexican government and Santa Anna himself repudiated the treaty, Texas won its independence and Santa Anna lost credibility.

The second set of events involved the Mexican-American War of 1846–1848. Having regained power (after the war began

POLK AND THE OREGON QUESTION

Polk also faced difficulties related to Oregon. The United States and Great Britain held joint control of the territory and had done so since 1818. Although he had promised to expand U.S. control in Oregon as a candidate, Polk found it difficult to

to go badly for Mexico in 1847), Santa Anna waged an effective war against the United States. When Mexico City fell to American forces in September 1847, however, Santa Anna faced the unpleasant and impossible task of negotiating a treaty while a foreign army occupied his country. The 1848 Treaty of Guadalupe Hidalgo ended the war and drove Santa Anna from power. This treaty did not please many people in Mexico. Following the war, the Mexican government banished Santa Anna from the country. Later unrest led to Santa Anna's return to Mexico and to power, however.

Finally, Santa Anna was in power in 1853, when Mexico sold the Gadsden Purchase to the United States. Allegations of corruption clouded the deal, especially after full payment failed to reach Mexico. This scandal forced Santa Anna from office. Thus, "The dominant figure in Mexican politics for much of the nineteenth century, Antonio López de Santa Anna left a legacy of disappointment and disaster by consistently placing his own self-interest above his duty to the nation."[*] Santa Anna never again held political office. He died in 1876.

*PBS. "Antonio Lopez de Santa Anna," New Perspectives on the West. Available online at http://www.pbs.org/weta/thewest/people/s_z/santa-anna.htm.

carry through on his pledge. When war broke out with Mexico in 1846, Polk decided to end the possibility of another conflict. Diplomatic efforts led to an 1848 treaty that resolved the issue of Oregon.

The treaty established the border between the United States and Canada at the 49th Parallel. Although Polk wisely settled the dispute rather than risk a war with Great Britain, the terms did not conform to his campaign pledge to fight for a border at 56°40'. In August 1848, the United States organized its piece of Oregon into the Oregon Territory.

The War
with Mexico

The influx of American settlers into lands claimed by Mexico led to increased tensions between Mexico and the United States. Following the Texans' 1836 victory at San Jacinto, Mexico tried twice to recover Texas. Both endeavors fell short. Despite these failures, Mexico still insisted that Texas was Mexican territory. The Mexican government notified the United States that American annexation of Texas would be grounds for war.

Whether the United States desired Texas was not in question. Twice, the United States had offered to purchase Texas from Mexico. Both times, Mexico had rebuffed the offers. The first purchase request came in 1827, when President John Quincy Adams offered Mexico $1 million for the territory. Adams's successor, Andrew Jackson, increased the offer to $5 million in 1829. Again, Mexico refused to sell. Still, Spain's attempts to retake Mexico and America's interest in Texas convinced Mexican officials that the large number of American immigrants in Texas might pose a problem.

After gaining independence, Texas adopted a constitution that recognized slavery as legal. Texas then applied for admittance to the Union, but the slavery issue stirred up passions in the United States. An additional slave state promised to strengthen the power of the less populous slave-holding Southern states in the federal government. Efforts to annex Texas and admit it as a state failed in 1837. The Republic of Texas then sought recognition as a sovereign state. In 1838, it received such recognition from Great Britain and the United States. Texas remained an independent republic until after the 1844 American presidential election.

When Texas became the twenty-eighth state in 1845, Mexico stopped short of declaring war. Instead, Mexico responded by breaking off diplomatic ties with the United States and sending the American diplomat back to Washington, D.C. President Polk prepared for a possible war. Polk developed both diplomatic and war strategies. He drew up plans to avoid war by offering compensation to Mexico for lands in the American southwest and to settle the Texas question. Polk also directed American forces into Texas, however, and sent American ships to the Gulf of Mexico. The ships remained in the Gulf until the outbreak of war.

DIPLOMATIC FAILURE

In November 1845, President Polk appointed James Slidell as ambassador to Mexico in an attempt to purchase the Mexican territories of Alta California and Santa Fé de Nuevo México (the California and New Mexico territories). Slidell was a Democrat from Louisiana. He had served one term in the U.S. House of Representatives, and he spoke fluent Spanish. Slidell traveled south and arrived in Mexico City in 1845. The situation was not encouraging. Because the Mexican government suffered from instability, no leader could maintain power effectively for very long. As a result, no Mexican leader was willing to negotiate with the Americans and risk losing what little influence he had. When Mexican president José Joaquín de Herrera merely considered meeting with Slidell to negotiate a peaceful solution regarding the Texas annexation, his opponents accused him of treason and removed him from power.

After the removal of Herrera, General Mariano Paredes y Arrillaga was named president on January 3, 1845. He offered his countrymen a more patriotic regime and openly claimed that Texas belonged to Mexico. Mexican authorities continued to make Slidell wait. After almost six months in Mexico, no Mexican official had yet met with him to discuss the American offer to purchase Alta California and Santa Fé de Nuevo México. Slidell became convinced that he could not fulfill his mission. He returned to the United States.

The diplomatic snub given to Slidell persuaded Polk that war with Mexico was the only way to deal with the issue. In April 1846, Polk met with his cabinet and recommended that the United States "take the remedy for the injuries and wrongs we had suffered into our own hands."[1] The cabinet voiced its approval, and Polk began to draft a message asking Congress to declare war. The president had little justification beyond Mexico's refusal to accept his offer to buy the California and New Mexico territories and the Mexican government's refusal to pay debts owed to American citizens. Fortunately for Polk, events soon took place that gave him the excuse he needed to prod Congress to declare war. Those events were centered on competing views of the Texas border.

A BOUNDARY DISPUTE

Despite America's annexation of Texas in 1845, the Mexican and American governments continued to quarrel over ownership claims to Texas. A larger issue, however, centered on the location of the southern border of Texas. The United States argued that the Rio Grande was the boundary, a claim that was bolstered by an 1836 treaty. Mexico insisted that Texas extended only to the Nueces River, which ran about 150 miles north of the Rio Grande. The United States argued that the Rio Grande was the actual boundary, a claim bolstered by an 1836 treaty. Because Mexico had never ratified the 1836 treaty, it understandably maintained that the Mexico-Texas border was farther north, at the Nueces.

In January 1846, President Polk dispatched General Zachary Taylor and a sizeable force of 3,000 men to secure the border. Taylor proceeded to the Rio Grande, paying no attention to Mexican demands to pull back to the Nueces. Across the Rio Grande from the Mexican settlement of Matamoros, Taylor erected a crude defensive structure, later named Fort Texas. The presence of the American troops angered many Mexicans, and Mexican general Mariano Arista readied his forces for war.

Some historians believe that Polk tried to instigate a war. Others believe that the president sent troops to Texas to prevent a possible conflict. Regardless of Polk's intentions, the presence of a large U.S. force within disputed territory led to a skirmish, and that skirmish resulted in a large-scale armed conflict with Mexico.

A key incident occurred on April 24, 1846. A large Mexican cavalry unit crossed the Rio Grande into the disputed territory between the Rio Grande and the Nueces. There the Mexicans engaged an American patrol of 63 men led by Captain Seth Thornton. The Mexican cavalry routed the American patrol, which suffered 11 dead, including the commanding officer. Although the Mexican force captured most of the other Americans, a few managed to escape back to Fort Texas. Polk took advantage of the event, later known as the Thornton Skirmish or the Thornton Affair, and used it as evidence to persuade Congress to declare war against Mexico on May 13, 1846.

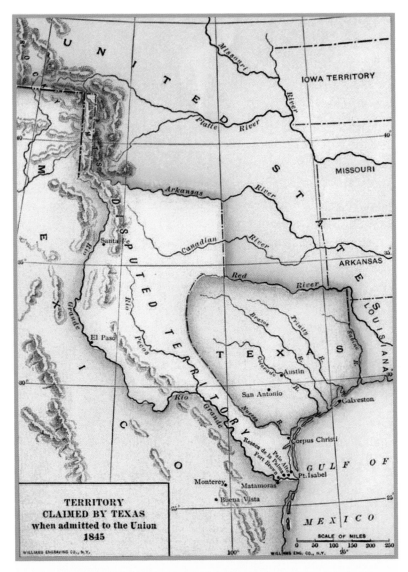

TERRITORY
CLAIMED BY TEXAS
when admitted to the Union
1845

Although Texas was admitted to the Union in 1845, its boundaries continued to be in dispute. Mexico claimed the Nueces River, north of the Rio Grande, as its border with Texas, while the United States claimed it was the Rio Grande. In response, Congress approved President Polk's declaration of war, which the Southern Democrats saw as an opportunity to expand the number of slave states.

WAR!

On May 11, 1846, President James Polk asked Congress to declare war against Mexico. In his message, Polk declared, "Mexico has passed the boundary of the United States, has invaded our territory and shed American blood upon the American soil. She has proclaimed that hostilities have commenced, and that the two nations are now at war."[2] The president then urged Congress and the United States to take up arms, saying that Americans "are called upon by every consideration of duty and patriotism to vindicate with decision the honor, the rights, and the interests of our country."[3]

Congress debated the measure, which the Whigs harshly criticized. Much of their opposition rested on the likelihood that war would result in additional slave states. If the United States acquired land from Mexico, it would likely be the vast regions west of Texas. Since slavery had already expanded into Texas, Northern Whigs feared that these territories would allow slave interests to expand their economic and political power. In the end, however, the declaration passed overwhelmingly on May 13, 1846. Fourteen Whigs cast no votes. Two of those 14 were a former president and a future president, John Quincy Adams and Abraham Lincoln. Mexico belatedly followed suit. Their congress declared war on July 7. The United States went eagerly to war, and Polk appointed General Zachary Taylor to lead the American forces.

"OLD ROUGH AND READY"

Zachary Taylor appeared to be the perfect commander of the American forces. Nicknamed "Old Rough and Ready" because of his customary straw hat and scruffy appearance, Taylor had proved his abilities fighting American Indians during the War of 1812, the Black Hawk War, and the Second Seminole War. The general turned his attention to securing his position and shoring up his defenses. The 3,000 American troops pieced together fortifications, which Taylor named Fort Texas. This fort relied on supplies from the Gulf Coast, located about 40 miles inland on Point Isabel.

Meanwhile, General Arista waited with 4,000 soldiers at Matamoros, across the Rio Grande from Taylor's position. To drive the Americans from that position, Arista ordered an artillery attack on Fort Texas as he simultaneously crossed the river with the bulk of his army. The Mexican force now threatened to cut off Taylor from his supply base. On May 1, Taylor and the main part of his force avoided Arista's maneuver and escaped to Point Isabel. There, the Americans collected reinforcements and needed supplies before heading back west to aid the defenders left in Fort Texas. Arista continued his attack and positioned 3,400 men between Taylor and Fort Texas, at a place called Palo Alto, just north of the fort.

The ensuing battle, fought on May 8, 1846, was the first major battle of the Mexican-American War. Taylor, with 2,200 men, faced the waiting Mexicans. The Americans effectively used their artillery to batter the Mexican force. The advanced tactics employed by the Americans prevented the Mexicans from using their larger numbers or their sizable cavalry to their best advantage. The battle raged until dark, at which point Arista withdrew his men to a more defensible position at Resaca de la Palma. Arista had suffered about 250 to 400 casualties, and the Americans had lost about half as many.

On May 9, the two armies clashed again, this time at Resaca de la Palma. Taylor's forces drove the Mexicans from the field. Arista and his forces escaped across the Rio Grande. Taylor then returned to Fort Texas, where he discovered that its commander, Major Jacob Brown, was dead. In honor of the fallen commander, Taylor renamed the installation Fort Brown. Today, it is the site of Brownsville, Texas. Old Rough and Ready had helped to establish and maintain the U.S. position in Texas.

GEN. TAYLOR AT THE BATTLE OF PALO ALTO.

The Battle of Palo Alto was the first major battle of the Mexican-American War. General Zachary Taylor (on horse) and a force of 2,400 troops fought Mexico's force of 3,400 over the U.S. Army installation Fort Texas, which the Mexicans viewed as being on Mexican land. Mexican forces suffered large casualties compared to the Americans, spurring a significant morale boost across the United States.

MONTERREY

After losing to the Americans, General Arista withdrew from the settlement of Matamoros. A few weeks later, Taylor and his men crossed the Rio Grande and occupied the settlement. Not wanting to create future problems for himself and his troops, Taylor ordered his men to leave the local citizens alone. After restocking their supplies, the U.S. forces boarded boats and headed west, up the Rio Grande. When he arrived at the town of Camargo, Taylor waited for coming reinforcements. His forces swelled to 12,000 men, but disease claimed the lives of about 1,500 of them. Bored with the inaction and subjected to disease, American soldiers called Camargo "a Yawning Graveyard."[4]

In early September 1846, the American forces left Camargo. Taylor now set his sights on the city of Monterrey. To occupy northern Mexico, the United States needed to capture this city. After seizing the road to Saltillo (the capital of Texas before the Texas Revolution), the only escape route for the Mexican force, the Americans set out to capture Monterrey. General Pedro Ampudia had replaced Arista as commander following the Mexican defeat at Resaca de la Palma. Taylor's forces outnumbered Ampudia's. Taylor had more than 6,400 men; Ampudia had 5,000. Although Ampudia held secure defensive positions, there was no hope of reinforcements or supplies reaching the city's defenders.

On September 21, Taylor launched a two-sided attack. One American force came from the east and one from the west-southwest side of Monterrey. Both assaults pushed the defenders back, forcing them to withdraw to the center of the city. There, the Mexican forces braced themselves for the coming attack. They holed up in houses, in the cathedral, and in a stronghold called the Black Fort. On September 23, after a one-day respite, the American attack resumed. The U.S. forces made inroads into the Mexican defenses, but darkness forced them to halt their advance. On September 24, with the United States prevailing, Taylor ordered his artillery to begin shelling what remained of the Mexican forces. Ampudia asked for a cease-fire to discuss terms. The United States and Mexico each had lost about 450 men in the battle.

Under the negotiated terms, Taylor unwisely allowed Ampudia and his remaining men to leave the city with some of their arms. Additionally, the two sides agreed to a cessation of hostilities for two months. Taylor's officers supported his decision, as additional fighting promised to be fierce and costly.

The victory at Monterrey was an important turning point in the war. The agreement that allowed the Mexican army to withdraw angered the American commander–in–chief, however. President Polk was convinced that Taylor could not be trusted. Having lost the president's confidence, Taylor lost what little influence he had in shaping the war's strategy.

SANTA ANNA RETURNS

Polk poured most of his efforts into securing a settled peace through negotiation with an unlikely figure: former Mexican president Antonio López de Santa Anna, who had lost power in 1844. Corruption under Santa Anna's leadership had led to his exile to Cuba. Despite his circumstances, however, Santa Anna never gave up hope of ruling Mexico again. In February 1846, as tensions between Mexico and the United States grew and war clouds gathered, Santa Anna sent a representative, Colonel Alejandro J. Atocha, to President Polk. Colonel Atocha communicated Santa Anna's desire to return to power. The U.S. Navy had blockaded the Mexican coast, preventing Santa Anna from returning to Mexico. If the United States allowed Santa Anna to return to Mexico, he might be able to regain power. If he regained power, he promised to cooperate with Polk and end the war through a negotiated treaty. Apparently, Santa Anna offered to cede Mexico's claims to northern California, New Mexico, and Texas to the United States in exchange for $30 million.

Santa Anna's offer placed Polk in a difficult situation and forced him to plot a course around several issues. First, Santa Anna was in exile. He had no authority to negotiate anything with any country on behalf of Mexico. Second, Santa Anna had a reputation as anything but trustworthy. If Santa Anna returned to Mexico, there were no guarantees that he would keep his word. Third, to escort such a man—with his military training and experience—back to Mexico while Mexico was at war with the United States was potentially dangerous. Despite these concerns, Polk agreed to let Santa Anna return to Mexico.

Antonio López de Santa Anna returned to Mexico City in September 1846, at about the time that Taylor's forces captured the city of Monterrey. As soon as Santa Anna returned, he set about gaining control and shoring up his country's defenses. As soon as he could manage to, he headed north to face Taylor. Santa Anna collected a force of over 20,000 men and met Taylor at the pass near Hacienda de Buena Vista. Taylor's forces shored up their defenses within the hills and gullies of the area's rugged terrain.

On February 22, 1847, the two armies engaged in light clashes. The next day, Santa Anna threw the weight of his forces at the American defenders. The battle was fierce, and it seemed as though Taylor and his troops were in danger of being driven from the field. Taylor's second in command, General John E. Wool, reported, "General, we are whipped." Taylor rejected the assessment and responded, "That is for me to determine."[5] After calling up reinforcements, the Americans managed to hold their line throughout the day. The next morning, Santa Anna and his army were gone. The Mexicans retreated to Mexico City. Taylor and his men had survived the onslaught. American forces continued their occupation of northern Mexico.

SCOTT TAKES CONTROL

Zachary Taylor's successes resulted in national acclaim, and Polk began to fear Taylor as a rival for the presidency. The fact that the now-popular general was a member of the Whig Party did little to help his standing with the president. Polk believed that Taylor was a threat to his presidency. This view led the commander–in–chief to favor alternative military maneuvers that did not include Taylor.

Thus, General Winfield Scott led a second army into Mexico in March 1847. Ships of the U.S. Navy carried Scott's army of 12,000 men to Veracruz, Mexico; the troops' disembarkation marked the first large amphibious landing ever conducted by American forces. On March 9, 1847, Scott laid siege to Veracruz. During the fight, American soldiers began to fall victim to yellow fever. Despite this setback, the city surrendered 12 days later. The Mexicans suffered about 180 killed and wounded, compared with about 80 Americans.

From Veracruz, Scott launched an invasion into the heart of Mexico with approximately 8,500 healthy men. Santa Anna established defensive positions with 12,000 men about halfway between Veracruz and Mexico City, near a mountain pass called

POLK'S WAR MESSAGE

In his May 11, 1846, message to Congress, President James K. Polk made several claims to justify the declaration of war against Mexico. Critics later challenged the president's version of events, portraying Polk as a warmonger intent on waging a war of expansion. Detractors disputed Polk's contention that the attack by Mexican forces—the Thornton Skirmish—had taken place on American soil. The site of the attack was, in fact, a disputed area. Both Texas and Mexico claimed the territory. Whigs and other opponents of the president disputed Polk's words, claiming that he had twisted the truth to win support for a war declaration.

Despite its detractors, Polk's war message effectively gained the president congressional support for the declaration of war against Mexico. Polk made his case to Congress and to the American people. In the end, Polk's war message set the stage for the United States to wage a successful war. The war message demonstrated Polk's political ability to maneuver through and around events to reach his goals. During the war, the United States crossed the Mexican border and shed Mexican blood on Mexican soil. As a result of the war, the United States greatly expanded its territorial holdings. Here are some of Polk's words to Congress on that fateful day in May:

Cerro Gordo. Santa Anna fortified this canyon, which over-looked the most important roadway to the capital.

The Mexican force held the high ground and trained their artillery on the road below. Scott sent his mounted heavy cavalry, which made up about a third of his force, ahead of the main body of troops. The Mexican artillery opened fire on the cavalry, losing the element of surprise. Because Scott realized

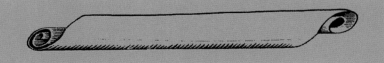

. . . we have been exerting our best efforts to propitiate her good will. Upon the pretext that Texas, a nation as independent as herself, thought proper to unite its destinies with our own she has affected to believe that we have severed her rightful territory, and in official proclamations and manifestoes has repeatedly threatened to make war upon us for the purpose of reconquering Texas. In the meantime we have tried every effort at reconciliation. The cup of forbearance had been exhausted even before the recent information from the frontier of the Del Norte. But now, after reiterated menaces, Mexico has passed the boundary of the United States, has invaded our territory and shed American blood upon the American soil. She has proclaimed that hostilities have commenced, and that the two nations are now at war.

As war exists, and, notwithstanding all our efforts to avoid it, exists by the act of Mexico herself, we are called upon by every consideration of duty and patriotism to vindicate with decision the honor, the rights, and the interests of our country.[*]

* *"Message of President Polk," The Avalon Project at Yale Law School. Available online at http://www.yale.edu/lawweb/avalon/presiden/ messages/polk01.htm.*

In early March 1847, thousands of U.S. troops landed on the beaches south of Veracruz during the first large-scale amphibious assault conducted by U.S. military forces. U.S. forces occupied this Mexican seaport for 20 days, and the Mexican forces surrendered, opening up the east coast of Mexico to the United States.

that he could not defeat Santa Anna in the canyon, he circumvented the Mexican position by marching northward through rough terrain. Scott positioned his artillery on even higher ground, above the Mexican defenses. Scott's attacking force also had outflanked the Mexican defenders. Santa Anna and his men did not understand the seriousness of the situation until it was too late. The U.S. forces attacked and routed the Mexicans, killing and wounding approximately 1,000 men and capturing another 3,000.

On May 1, the city of Puebla surrendered peacefully to Scott. Puebla was situated in a high, broad valley about 60 miles

(96 kilometers) southeast of Mexico City. Puebla was the second-largest city in Mexico, and many of its residents were unfriendly to Santa Anna and his regime. After several more skirmishes and battles, on September 13, 1847, Scott attacked the castle at Chapultepec, on a high point west of Mexico City. The U.S. forces drove the Mexicans back from Chapultepec, thereby leaving the capital unprotected. Scott's army entered Mexico City the next day. Militarily, the United States had won the war. Diplomatic wrangling dictated the terms of peace, however. The United States hailed Scott as a hero for his successes, and he served as military governor of Mexico City while American forces occupied the capital.

The Fruits
of War

Despite its popularity, the war with Mexico did have some detractors. To begin with, not everyone agreed with the version of events that Polk set forth in his war message. Some people did not care for the idea of the United States expanding through military conquest. Still others feared that the war was nothing more than a means by which the slave-holding South could extend slavery and increase the region's national power within the federal government.

OPPOSITION TO THE WAR

Generally, most Whigs opposed the war, and most Democrats supported it. Many high-profile objections and statements were made against the war. One member of Congress, Joshua Reed Giddings of Ohio, created a stir by calling the conflict "an aggressive, unholy, and unjust war."[1] He defended his vote against the war, declaring, "In the murder of Mexicans upon their own soil, or in robbing them of their country, I can take no part now or hereafter. The guilt of these crimes must rest on others—I will not participate in them . . ."[2] Giddings compared his vote to those of the British Whigs who refused to support measures supplying the British war effort against the Americans in 1776. Writer Henry David Thoreau refused to pay taxes; he claimed that to do so offered support to a war that he opposed. Authorities placed Thoreau in jail, where he put the time to good use by writing his essay *Civil Disobedience*. In it, Thoreau argued that an individual should bow to his or her conscience, not to the power of the government.

One prominent Whig, Daniel D. Barnard, recorded his opposition to the war in writing. "We support the country," Barnard wrote, "though we do not support the administration; we support the war, though we condemn those who have brought us into it."[3] A lesser known—at that time—freshman member of Congress from the state of Illinois showed no fear as he stood up to the president. Abraham Lincoln offered what became known as his "Spot Resolutions." In them, Lincoln demanded to see the exact "spot" where American blood was spilled. The freshman Whig questioned Polk's claim that Mexicans had drawn American blood on American soil. Lincoln charged, "That soil was not ours; and Congress did not annex or attempt to annex it."[4] Lincoln went further, maintaining, "It is a fact, that the United States Army, in marching to the Rio Grande, marched into a peaceful Mexican settlement, and frightened the inhabitants away from their homes and their growing crops."[5]

The Illinois representative voted in favor of a resolution that claimed Polk had violated the Constitution in starting the war and that called the conflict unnecessary. His political stance on the Mexican-American War cost Lincoln dearly. An Illinois newspaper dubbed him "spotty Lincoln."[6] The future president served only one term in the House, choosing not to run for reelection in the face of popular support for the war.

Others from within his own party opposed Polk, although not as openly as did many of the Whigs. Democrat John C. Calhoun proved to be a possible foe, and Polk took great pains to maintain good relations with the powerful senator from South Carolina. Calhoun did not openly oppose the war. He questioned the necessity of sending American troops deep into Mexico, however. Opponents argued that because the president claimed that the war was essential to protect the Texas-Mexico border, the invasion of Mexico was unnecessary. Through intermediaries, Polk politely listened to Calhoun's argument and delayed before rejecting the call to withdraw all troops back to Texas. The other South Carolinian senator, Andrew Butler, understood the dilemma facing Polk. He commented, "If we quit the war, it will be apparently with dishonor. If we go on, it must end in mischief. The truth is, we are like the shepherd who has got the wolf by the ears! It is hazardous to let go—it is worse to hold on."[7] Indeed, the matter of war with Mexico was hazardous, and Polk continued to receive criticism from all sides about his handling of the war and the acquisition of territory.

Critics also reminded Polk of his campaign pledge of "Fifty-four forty or fight" to settle the dispute with Great Britain over Oregon. Polk had run on a pro-expansion platform, in which he promised to bring Texas into the Union. Polk had never discussed war with Mexico during the campaign, however. Political opponents expressed outrage over Polk's willingness to compromise with Great Britain by reducing American territorial demands for free territory in the Northwest even as he waged a war to expand potential slave territory in the South. To some Northern Whigs, Polk seemed intent on expanding slave-state power and limiting the power of free states.

Whigs condemned Polk's war message, calling it "a vile attempt to cover up the grossest act of usurpation and aggression

John C. Calhoun (1782–1850), who had approved the annexation of Texas, was deeply fearful that doubling the nation's size by attacking Mexico would turn the balance of power in the Senate forever against the South. He wanted the Union to be for whites only, and incorporating Mexico into the United States meant welcoming nonwhites.

by the President known to the history of the country."[8] One Whig member of Congress insisted that the annexation of Texas was an indirect cause of the war and Polk's insistence on occupying disputed territory with federal troops was the direct cause. These and other protests received attention in the press and sparked debate. It was a relatively unknown member of Congress from the president's own party, however, who ignited the firestorm that forever cast a shadow on the Mexican War. That congressman was David Wilmot.

THE WILMOT PROVISO

David Wilmot introduced his amendment, later called the Wilmot Proviso, in August 1848. This amendment did not oppose the war, but it did limit what the United States could achieve through it. Specifically, the proviso banned slavery in any lands or territory that the United States gained in the war. This amendment was the first attempt in the Congress of the United States to legislate the political ideology of opposition to the extension of slavery. The amendment did not seek to alter the existence of slavery where it already was established. It did, however, seek to limit slavery by restricting where American citizens might introduce or establish it.

To Polk and many Southerners, the proviso was nothing short of an attack on the property rights of American citizens. After the bill to which the proviso was an amendment failed to pass, Polk and others angrily denounced the proviso as divisive and unconstitutional. As explained in the first chapter, how-ever, the Wilmot Proviso never really went away. Instead, the issues that Wilmot introduced remained central to American politics through the Civil War.

NEW MEXICO AND CALIFORNIA

In 1846, the United States set out to win the Mexican-American War and gain the territory that Polk had attempted to purchase from Mexico. To do this, the United States initially opened two major fronts against Mexico. Colonel Stephen Kearny was stationed in Fort Leavenworth, in present-day Kansas. Kearny received orders to head west and occupy California to pre-vent Great Britain from establishing a presence there. At the Pacific coast, Kearny was to meet up with an American fleet commanded by Commodore John Drake Sloat. On the second front, two armies were ordered to march southward, directly into Mexico. One army was commanded by General Zachary Taylor; the other, by General John E. Wool.

After the outbreak of war, during the summer of 1846, Stephen Kearny led his force south and west to Santa Fe, New Mexico. Along the way, Kearny encountered New Mexico residents who desired to rid themselves of Mexican rule. The Mexican government had mostly overlooked the province, and many within it welcomed the invading American force. Kearny and his men faced no resistance when they entered the city of Santa Fe on August 15, 1846. The United States now held New Mexico.

With Santa Fe secure, Kearny turned his attention to California. Leading his men west, Kearny encountered Kit Carson, the famed western guide. Carson informed Kearny that the United States already had gained control of California. In view of Carson's words, and because the remainder of the trail west passed through the desert and promised to be harsh, Kearny continued with only two companies of men and sent the balance of his troops back to Santa Fe.

Unfortunately, Carson's report was incomplete and outdated. The Americans had indeed seized California, but Mexican residents were in open rebellion against the occupying forces. Kearny discovered this before he arrived in California, but after he sent the bulk of his force back to Santa Fe. On December 2, 1846, the Americans reached Warner's Ranch, outside San Diego, California. A Mexican force much larger than his own awaited Kearny near an American Indian village called San Pasqual, in present-day San Diego County, in southern California.

Despite the odds against him, Kearny acted boldly. Even though the long march had taken its toll on his men, Kearny decided to attack the larger Mexican contingent with his fatigued force. American captain Benjamin Moore led an ill-fated saber charge. The Mexicans nearly routed the Americans, but Kearny's men were spared from a thorough defeat by the timely arrival of reinforcements and artillery. The American forces finally won the battle, but they lost 18 men, including Moore.

On December 11, 1846, Kearny led his men into San Diego. Once there, they combined forces with Commodore Robert Stockton and his marines. Together, they suppressed the residents' uprising. In doing so, they secured California. The United States maintained control of California for the remainder of the war, and the final peace treaty recognized American ownership of California.

THE BEAR REPUBLIC

On June 15, 1846, in northern California, about 30 settlers, mostly American and all non-Mexican, engineered a revolt against the Mexican garrison at Sonoma. These insurgents raised the so-called Bear Flag and proclaimed the California Republic. The Bear Flag featured the words "California Republic" as well as images of a star and bear. The rebels did not know that the United States and Mexico already were at war.

After declaring themselves independent, the rebels arrested General Mariano Guadalupe Vellejo, the former Mexican commander of northern California. The men viewed Vellejo as a threat because he led a private military unit and had ties to the Mexican government. The men sent Vellejo to Sutter's Fort and held him there until August 1. The rebels also quickly named William B. Ide as president of the new republic. The Bear Flag revolt successfully began the process of winning California's independence from Mexico. The new government waited for others to join in the revolt and for the inevitable Mexican reaction. They did not have to wait long.

American lieutenant colonel John C. Frémont arrived in the area on June 23 with 60 soldiers and took command of the entire rebel force. By this time, the Mexican governor and

On June 14, 1846, American officer John C. Frémont (1813–1890) and a group of insurgents seized the Mexican fort at Sonoma and proclaimed California an independent republic. Once they were informed that the Mexican-American War had begun, they abandoned their plans and joined the fight to make California a state. They replaced the Bear Flag with the Stars and Stripes.

general, José Castro, recognized that the threat was serious. Castro answered the insurgents' challenge by sending 50 soldiers to attack the rebels. The defenders soundly defeated the Mexican force in the Battle of Olompali on June 24, 1846.

Three naval vessels commanded by John D. Sloat defeated the Mexican force at Monterey, California, on July 7. Sloat then informed Frémont that the United States was at war with Mexico. The brief existence of the California Republic ended as the rebels tore down the Bear Flag and raised the American flag. The rebellion against Mexican rule turned into a fight to be included in the United States. After serving just 25 days as the only president of the California Republic, William Ide stepped down to take his place as a private in the U.S. Army under Frémont.

The Mexican-American War in California was over. On January 16, 1847, Commodore Robert F. Stockton appointed Lieutenant Colonel Frémont military governor of California. Unfortunately, professional jealousy created problems between General Kearny and Lieutenant Colonel Frémont. Kearny outranked Frémont. Because of this, Kearny decided that the role of military governor should belong to the highest-ranking officer. Kearny arrested Frémont and shipped him east to Washington, D.C., to stand trial for mutiny. The military court convicted Frémont, but because of his accomplishments in the war, President Polk swiftly pardoned him. Frémont later served as a California senator and won nomination as the first presidential candidate of the Republican Party in 1856.

For President Polk and the American military, all attention now turned toward the war in Mexico. Some expansionists began to demand something new and bigger from the war with Mexico. These war supporters insisted that the United States take all of Mexico to democratize an even larger region than either Texas or New Mexico and California. President Polk now faced opposition from both sides of the argument: from those who opposed the United States expanding its territory through war and from those who now favored greatly enlarging territorial gains by armed force. The issue, although a thorny one, was not a new one to Polk or to his inner circle. In fact, the president already had made a decision regarding territorial expansion in the event of war with Mexico.

"ALL MEXICO"

On the day that Congress declared war against Mexico, President Polk and his cabinet contemplated the subject of acquiring territory through conquest. Secretary of State James Buchanan raised the issue, suggesting that the United States announce the purpose of the war as self-defense rather than territorial expansion. Polk immediately disagreed. He believed that such a statement "would be improper and unnecessary."[9] The president agreed that the war was not being waged for conquest. As he noted, however, "yet it was clear that in making peace we would if practicable obtain California and such other portion of the Mexican territory as would be sufficient to indemnify our claimants on Mexico and to defray the costs of the war."[10] In other words, Polk seemingly wanted to project the image of a war without conquest even as he wanted to reap all the benefits of conquest in the negotiated peace at the conclusion of the war. Buchanan lost the argument, and the United States made no declaration against acquiring land from Mexico.

The idea of a gaining land through armed conflict had little support. Even editor John O'Sullivan, who first published the term *Manifest Destiny,* "always emphasized the view that no people or state ever entered the Union except of their own free choice."[11] The concept that Americans would compel others into the nation went against the very ideals of self-government. When the war began, however, even many of those who had staunchly opposed the war supported expansion as the opportunity presented itself. Even Abraham Lincoln voted in favor of receiving territory from Mexico. Despite the sudden wave of support for expansion, the shift in public sentiment raised new issues and created sharp political divisions.

Soon after the war began, a faction grew within the Democratic Party that supported acquiring all of Mexico. The members of this "All Mexico" movement fervently demanded that the war continue until the United States controlled all of Mexico. The emergence of this expansionist group led to a political backlash. Specifically, abolitionists—those who favored ending slavery in the United States—accused the Democrats of satisfying Southern demands for new slave territories. The All Mexico demands contributed to the ongoing furor over the Wilmot Proviso.

Polk faced a potentially disastrous political situation. Some of his most ardent supporters demanded that he conduct the war even more forcefully. At the same time, his critics charged that he was too aggressive. The situation seemed hopeless, but Polk saw the opportunity to accomplish his primary goal of expanding American territory. Because both sides wanted more, Polk took the middle ground. He appeared to offer a compromise; in fact, however, he succeeded in realizing his initial war aims. All that Polk needed, as the war moved toward its conclusion, was a completed peace treaty.

THE TREATY OF GUADALUPE-HIDALGO

In 1847 Polk sent Nicholas P. Trist as U.S. peace commissioner to conclude a treaty with Mexico. Trist arrived in Mexico City with a proposal that included several provisions: that Mexico recognize the Rio Grande as the border of Texas; that Mexico relinquish New Mexico and both Alta (upper) and Baja (lower) California; and that Mexico guarantee Americans the right of transit across the Tehuantepec isthmus (the narrowest band of Mexican land lying between the Gulf of Mexico and the Pacific Ocean). In return, the United States was willing to compensate Mexico up to $20 million for the lands being ceded and about $3 million more to settle claims of U.S. citizens against Mexico.

The negotiations took longer than expected. Trist tried diligently to negotiate with Mexican leaders, but American victories shook the Mexican government and made it virtually impossible to continue negotiations. Scott's capture of Mexico City in mid-September disrupted the negotiations as Santa Anna and all other high officials fled the capital.

At this point, Polk feared that Trist was incapable of obtaining an ideal treaty. Despite the difficulties, Trist continued to work toward forging a peace agreement. In October 1847, Polk

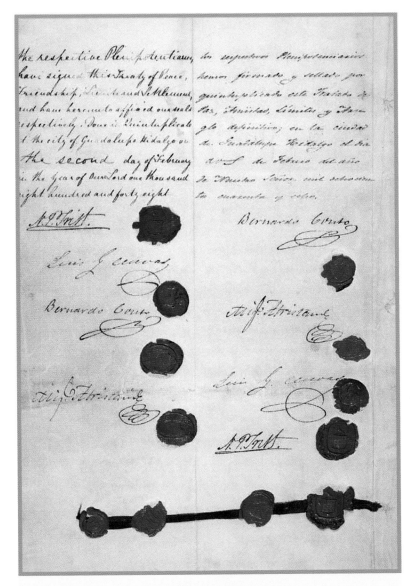

Pictured is the signed Treaty of Guadalupe Hidalgo, which ended the Mexican-American War and added more than 505,000 square miles to the United States. Mexico gave up all claims to the territory of Texas above the Rio Grande River and ceded New Mexico and California to the United States in exchange for $15 million.

recalled Trist to Washington, D.C. It took weeks for the president's message to reach Mexico City. Trist ignored the recall and remained in Mexico, convinced that he still could fulfill his mission and return with a favorable treaty. Finally, on February 2, 1848, Trist and his Mexican counterpart concluded their negotiations and signed the Treaty of Guadalupe Hidalgo.

The treaty officially ended the Mexican-American War. Under its terms, the United States received more than 500,000 square miles of territory. This acquisition of land positioned the United States to become a world power in the coming decades.

NICHOLAS TRIST
(1800–1874)

American Diplomat

In many ways, Nicholas Trist epitomized the American aristocracy. He was a native Virginian who was born into wealth. He was raised in Louisiana, studied and practiced law, married Thomas Jefferson's granddaughter, and served as private secretary to Andrew Jackson. Trist was a career government official who made a name for himself in governing circles.

In 1845, President James Polk appointed Trist chief clerk of the State Department. At the urging of Secretary of State James Buchanan, Polk then appointed Trist as his representative to negotiate a treaty to end the Mexican-American War. Trist arrived in Mexico City in April 1847. Negotiations moved slowly, in part because Mexican officials bickered among themselves as to who could negotiate. At one point, the Mexican negotiators fled before advancing American armies. Polk grew impatient with the slow progress of

RESULTS OF THE MEXICAN WAR

At first, little about the treaty satisfied President Polk. Nicholas Trist had violated direct orders to suspend negotiations. In addition, Trist had failed to secure all of Mexico, an unlikely demand that the president had become convinced was necessary. Trist, ever the crafty diplomat, shielded himself from Polk's anger by clinging to a set of presidential orders that commanded him to return to the United States with any treaty he might have signed. Thus, despite the tardy return of his envoy and the less than perfect terms of the treaty, Polk recognized that he finally had what he wanted: a treaty that

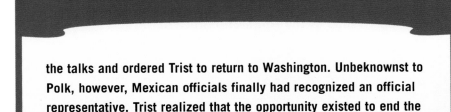

the talks and ordered Trist to return to Washington. Unbeknownst to Polk, however, Mexican officials finally had recognized an official representative. Trist realized that the opportunity existed to end the war and disregarded his recall orders. Pressing on, the two sides concluded the Treaty of Guadalupe-Hidalgo on February 2, 1848.

With his work done, Trist returned to Washington, D.C., with the treaty. Furious at the defiance of his representative, Polk fired Trist. In addition, the president refused to pay the negotiator for any work done after the initial recall date in October 1847.

Trist now faced the indignity of needing employment. He eventually found work with the Philadelphia, Wilmington, and Baltimore Railroad. He worked for the railroad until 1870, when he won appointment as postmaster of Alexandria, Virginia. The following year, Nicholas Trist finally received his back pay for negotiating the Treaty of Guadalupe Hidalgo. He died in 1874.

ended the war and secured vast amounts of territory from Mexico.

The United States benefited handsomely from the war. Mexico ceded all claims to the California, Utah, and New Mexico territories—more than 5 million square miles. Today, these lands make up much of the American Southwest, including all of California, Nevada, and Utah and parts of Wyoming, Colorado, Arizona, and New Mexico. In return, the United States agreed to pay $15 million to its vanquished neighbor. The U.S. government also guaranteed to protect specific rights of Mexicans living in the newly American territories. Mexico maintained both control over Baja California and access by land to that peninsula from the rest of Mexico. This was thanks, in part, to an obscure map that showed Baja California as separate from Alta California. Mexico agreed to recognize Texas as apart of the United States and accepted the American claim of the Rio Grande as the southern border of Texas. Finally, the United States agreed to pay Mexico $3.2 million in claims made by American citizens against the Mexican government. In all, after winning the war, the United States paid $18.2 million to Mexico in return for the territory America needed to fulfill its dream of Manifest Destiny.

Polk presented the treaty to the Senate for ratification. Critics on both sides disapproved of the measure. Some people wanted the United States to claim no land at all. Others still insisted that all of Mexico should come under U.S. control. The treaty appeared to offer a compromise, as it took some Mexican territory but left an independent Mexico in place.

In the end, Polk and the others recognized that the treaty accomplished nearly all of the aims of the war that were laid out when the hostilities began. To demand more after the fact was to risk not only intense public scrutiny but also justifiable attacks on the trustworthiness of the Polk administration. As the war and the negotiations had crawled on, public support had faded. Polk accepted this reality and threw his support behind the treaty. The Senate debates featured high emotions and brought about a few minor changes to the treaty. Ultimately, however, in March 1848, the Senate voted 38 to 14 in favor of ratification. The national legislature of Mexico ratified the slightly amended document in May. The Mexican-American War was finally over.

The Legacy of
Manifest Destiny

As a self-declared free society, the United States grappled with issues that stemmed from slavery from the moment the colonies declared their independence from Great Britain in 1776. A desire to realize the ideals of Manifest Destiny led Polk and other expansionists to wage war on Mexico. That war aroused passions and highlighted sectional differences that previous political generations had managed to sidestep. In the 1850s, after the Mexican-American War, the issue of slavery overshadowed virtually every major political issue. Slavery seemed to affect virtually every aspect of American life. This was especially true in matters related to western territories.

In 1850, the issue of slavery in the territories reared its head again. This time the matter was even more complex, as it involved more than just a single territory or state. The issue affected both the North and the South and developed into a crisis that threatened to tear apart the Union. The questions of California statehood and of territorial status for New Mexico and Utah sparked fierce political debates. Southern concerns about loopholes in the existing patchwork of local fugitive slave laws and distress about the ongoing slave trade in the nation's capital, Washington, D.C., only raised sensitivity to the debate. This set of complex and interrelated issues threatened to tear the nation apart. Leaders from both parties hoped to forge a political settlement to avert a civil war.

THE COMPROMISE OF 1850

On January 29, 1850, the venerable Henry Clay offered a compromise that he hoped would save the Union. Clay's compromise included elements favorable to both the North and the South. The plan included four main points. First, California would enter the Union as a free state. Second, the rest of the western territory gained in the war with Mexico would be partitioned along an east-west line into two territories (New Mexico and Utah) in which popular sovereignty would decide the issue of slavery. Third, a stricter fugitive slave law would require the return to their owners of any escaped slaves who were captured. Fourth, Congress would abolish the slave trade, but not slavery itself, in the District of Columbia, including the nation's capital city of Washington. The compromise was Henry Clay's last great political effort.

Two other aging statesmen also played roles in the crisis and compromise: John C. Calhoun and Daniel Webster. Although Calhoun was dying, he still served in the Senate. Sick and too weak to speak, he sat and listened as someone else read his speech to his colleagues, on March 4, 1850. The South Carolina senator's speech reminded the Senate that the South always had held a great deal of power in the federal government. Because the North had increased its power and influence in Washington through increased population, the South felt threatened by its inability to protect its region from federal power. Calhoun hinted that the South would leave the Union rather than allow the North to control the federal government.

Next, Daniel Webster rose to speak. Addressing the Senate, he uttered these unforgettable words, "I wish to speak today not as a Massachusetts man, nor as a Northern man, but as an American. . . . I speak today for the preservation of the Union. Hear me for my cause."[1] Webster favored compromise, a stance for which many in the North criticized him. Webster also warned the South, however. He declared that "there can be no such thing as a peaceable secession."[2] In Webster's mind, the South was in the Union and could only leave the Union through bloodshed.

All of this effort seemed to be wasted, however, as President Zachary Taylor promised to veto the bill. The president wanted the territories of California, Minnesota, New Mexico, Oregon, and Utah to receive statehood with no stipulations regarding their free or slave status. Because each of the potential states banned slavery, Taylor's proposal would have left the South with a 10-seat minority in the Senate. In July 1850, after debating the measure for eight months, with opposition from both the North and the South, the Senate killed the bill. It looked as though there was no chance for a compromise.

Then, without warning, the political environment changed overnight. President Taylor died, suddenly and unexpectedly, on July 9, 1850. Vice President Millard Fillmore, a 50-year-old Whig from New York, took the oath of office to become the thirteenth president of the United States. Because Fillmore supported a compromise, the chance to enact one existed again.

Henry Clay had led the fight for a compromise earlier in the summer. Leading the successful fight for compromise now fell to a new generation of leadership, however. This new generation was led by a Democrat from Illinois, Stephen Douglas. Because Douglas stood at a height of just 5 feet 4 inches, admirers and critics alike called him the Little Giant. Douglas recognized and understood the level of opposition that existed

Although Stephen A. Douglas (1813–1861) was an integral part of the Compromise of 1850, he reopened the debate on slavery with the highly controversial Kansas-Nebraska Act. The earlier compromises had settled the slavery issue, but this act allowed the new territories to decide for themselves whether or not to have slavery. The Republican Party was formed to stop this movement.

against various parts of the proposed compromise. To win passage, Douglas immediately separated each of the provisions of the original compromise into four separate bills. By doing this, he could build a distinct set of supporters willing to vote for each measure. Douglas also added a fifth bill that awarded $10 million to Texas to settle boundary disputes and territorial claims in the New Mexico Territory east of the Rio Grande.

Ultimately, the separate parts passed, but few members of Congress supported each bill of the so-called compromise. In many respects, the Compromise of 1850 gave the appearance of compromise and delivered the promised measures. In reality, however, the necessary maneuverings revealed the deep divide that existed within the country. Neither side had actually compromised with the other. Instead, each side had insured that the series of compromise bills gave it what it wanted and allowed the other side to claim its victories as well.

Fillmore signed the bills, and the Compromise of 1850 became law. This so-called compromise only submerged the troublesome issue of slavery, which had bubbled to the surface in the wake of the Mexican-American War. The rip currents of sectional divisiveness that swirled around the issue of slavery were stilled only in the maelstrom of the Civil War, more than a decade after the Compromise of 1850. Instead of drawing both sides together, the compromise revealed the deep fracture of the slavery issue. The so-called compromise also demonstrated how slavery threatened to divide the nation.

THE GADSDEN PURCHASE

The 1848 Treaty of Guadalupe Hidalgo did not end all disputes between Mexico and the United States and did not mark the end of America's acquisition of land from Mexico. Even after the Mexican-American War ended, the two countries continued to disagree over the exact location of a portion of the border. The United States wanted the disputed land west of the Rio Grande and south of the Gila River—land that today makes up the southern portions of Arizona and New Mexico—because it provided a more suitable right of way for a southern transcontinental railroad than undisputed American land just north of the border.

The idea of a southern transcontinental railroad was popular with many people in the South. Such a railroad could link the South with the Pacific, thereby increasing economic opportunities for the South. The prospect of a southern railroad also increased the likelihood that the Union might gain additional slave territories and future slave states. To realize their railroad dreams, Southern investors needed land south of the established border between the United States and Mexico.

In 1853, Secretary of War Jefferson Davis persuaded President Franklin Pierce to dispatch James Gadsden to Mexico to bargain with the Mexican government. A South Carolinian, Gadsden was a southern-railroad booster. Gadsden held shares in a company that planned to construct a railroad line connecting Texas with the Pacific coast. Evidently, this conflict of interest did not disqualify Gadsden from representing the Pierce administration as minister to Mexico.

Gadsden negotiated with Antonio de López de Santa Anna, the president of Mexico. The two reached an agreement on December 30, 1853. The United States agreed to pay $10 million for the disputed territory, a price of roughly 53 cents per acre. Controversy surrounded the payment, however. Although the agreement stipulated a $10 million payment, Congress appropriated only $7 million for the purchase. Inexplicably, when the payment arrived in the Mexican capital, $1 million was missing.

The Gadsden Purchase was the last adjoining North American territory acquired by the United States and incorporated into the nation's territory. (Alaska, which is separated from the rest of the continental United States by Canada, was purchased from Russia in 1867.) The sought-after southern railroad never materialized, however. As late as 1877, this was a political issue. In that year, Republican presidential candidate Rutherford B. Hayes agreed to support a southern route to end a national electoral dispute and secure his election to the presidency. Congress never approved funding for the project, however.

In 1853, the fiasco over the reduced payment and Mexican anger over the ceding of still more land to the United States led to the political demise of Santa Anna. Within months of the arrangement of the Gadsden Purchase, Santa Anna lost power for the eleventh and final time, and Mexico formed a new government. The territory ceded in the purchase belonged to the United States, however.

THE 1850S

In the election of 1852, the Whigs and the Democrats each offered a distinguished veteran of the Mexican-American War as a nominee. The Whigs nominated Winfield Scott, and the Democrats nominated Franklin Pierce. Despite Scott's popularity, the electorate chose Pierce as the fourteenth American president. During the Pierce administration, the issues that emerged in the war with Mexico continued to surface. The country was forced repeatedly to confront the issue of slavery. Because President Pierce favored expansion, the question of slavery in the territories never went away for long.

Another national leader, Illinois senator Stephen Douglas, wanted to see western lands opened up to allow the construction of a northern transcontinental railroad. Such a route would favor Douglas's adopted city of Chicago, Illinois. Douglas believed that the United States could continue to grow. "You cannot fix bounds to the onward march of this great and growing country. You cannot fetter the limbs of the young giant. He will burst all your chains. He will expand, and grow, and increase, and extend civilization, Christianity, and liberal principles."[3]

A key element to Douglas's vision of Manifest Destiny was a transcontinental railroad. Douglas used his influence, and construction began on a northern route. Two railroad companies, the Union Pacific and the Central Pacific, completed the project in May 1869, at Promontory Summit, Utah. The building of the last of the connecting routes was finished six months later. The first transcontinental railroad in the world was now in operation. It was a railroad whose very existence advanced the Manifest Destiny of the United States.

Shown is the ceremony of the First Transcontinental Railroad, marking the driving of the last spike, signifying the joining of the Central Pacific and the Union Pacific railroads on May 10, 1869, in Promontory Summit, Utah. Over six years, 1,756 miles of track was laid between Sacramento, California, and Omaha, Nebraska/Council Bluffs, Iowa. This railway network connected the Atlantic and Pacific coasts for the first time and was a vital link for the economy and population in the American West.

Americans looked for ways to increase settlement on the Great Plains. Once again, Stephen Douglas played a role in this development. With the Kansas-Nebraska Act of 1854, he sought to create two new territories. The act established the territories of Kansas and Nebraska and made the lands in those territories available for settlement. More importantly, the act also left it up to the settlers to decide the issue of slavery. To make this possible, the act included a repeal of the Missouri Compromise. That 1820 law had prohibited slavery north of 36°30' north latitude in the territory of the Louisiana Purchase.

THE KANSAS-NEBRASKA ACT OF 1854

In the 1840s, the Wilmot Proviso introduced the issue of slavery in the western territories to congressional debate. In 1854, the Kansas-Nebraska Act reintroduced the same issue but offered a solution. Stephen Douglas, the architect of the act, supported the concept of popular sovereignty. The Kansas-Nebraska Act divided the unsettled territory west of Missouri and Iowa into two separate territories, divided by the 40th parallel. The region south of that line became the Kansas Territory, and the region north of the parallel became the Nebraska Territory. Thus, both of the new territories (and potential future states) were either entirely or partially north of the 1820 Missouri Compromise line, which was set at 36°30' north.

The Kansas-Nebraska Act led many people on both sides of the slavery issue to take action. The result was a violent precursor to the Civil War that became known as Bleeding Kansas. In this conflict, which lasted from 1854 to 1858, slavery supporters from Missouri clashed with antislavery forces. Settlers in the Kansas Territory endured late-night raids, competing constitutions, and general anarchy. The turmoil prevented Kansas from entering the Union until January 1861, when it entered as a free state.

Why did Kansas become a focal point of violence for and against slavery? It did so because the Kansas-Nebraska Act of 1854 upset the political balance that had been in place since 1820. The act created two separate territories, a northern one and a southern one. The act also removed the north-of-the-parallel slavery ban

This provision of the Kansas-Nebraska Act provoked a political firestorm in the North. Critics condemned the law, claiming that the revocation of the slavery ban surrendered too much to the slave-holding South.

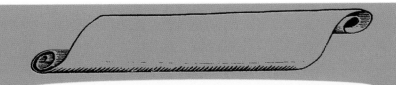

that the Missouri Compromise had set into place nearly three and a half decades before. Under the new act, the federal government no longer prohibited slavery in the region. Instead, "the said Territory or any portion of the same, shall be received into the Union with or without slavery, as their constitution may prescribe at the time of the admission."* The act goes on to say:

> *Be it enacted by the Senate and House of Representatives of the United States of America in Congress assembled*, That all that part of the territory of the United States . . . be . . . created into a temporary government by the name of the Territory Nebraska; and when admitted as a State or States, the said Territory or any portion of the same, shall be received into the Union with or without slavery, as their constitution may prescribe at the time of the admission. *And be it further enacted*, That all that part of the Territory of the United States . . . be . . . created into a temporary government by the name of the Territory of Kansas; and when admitted as a State or States, the said Territory, or any portion of the same, shall be received into the Union with or without slavery, as their Constitution may prescribe at the time of their admission."**

---

* "An Act to Organize the Territories of Nebraska and Kansas," The Avalon Project at Yale Law School. Available online at http://www.yale.edu/lawweb/avalon/kanneb.htm.
** Ibid.

Manifest Destiny opened a national debate about slavery. The debate about popular sovereignty paved the way for the formation of a new political party, a party with a strong anti-slavery leaning. The Whig Party splintered in the fight over slavery and fell apart in the wake of the Kansas-Nebraska Act. To fill the void, a new party emerged: the Republicans. The Republican Party picked up the standard of those who opposed the extension of slavery into the territories—especially those territories in which slavery had once been illegal. Almost immediately, the new party became the leading alternative to the Democrats in the North. The election in 1860 of the first Republican President, Abraham Lincoln, led directly to Southern secession and civil war.

MANIFEST DESTINY AFTER THE CIVIL WAR

After the North won the Civil War, the desire for American expansion did not subside. In 1867, Secretary of State William Seward negotiated with Russia to purchase Alaska. Under the agreement, the United States paid $7.2 million for Alaska, a price of about 2 cents per acre. Because Alaska was so far from other American holdings, and much of it had an Arctic climate, critics called it Seward's Folly. The acquisition insured, however, that no European power could establish a new foothold in North America. Later discoveries of gold and oil in addition to Alaska's other natural resources have only underlined the scope of Seward's vision in purchasing Alaska.

In the 1890s, the Spanish-American War epitomized the ideals of Manifest Destiny. The United States entered the war in defense of Cuban independence. America exited the war after gaining Puerto Rico in the Caribbean and the Philippines and Guam in the Pacific. Through this war, the United States also established itself as the dominant force in Cuba.

During the twentieth century, the United States continued to interject itself into the affairs of various Latin American countries. Presidents used expressions such as "Big Stick,"

"Dollar Diplomacy," and "Good Neighbor" to describe these foreign policy approaches. Regardless of the name, each of these foreign policies contained elements of Manifest Destiny. One of these elements was the idea that an infusion of American values and institutions can bring benefits to other nations.

The ideals of Manifest Destiny continued to influence the United States in sometimes surprising, sometimes subtle ways. When the United States entered World War I in 1917, it did so under the banner of making the world safe for democracy. Such idealism was a realization of America's perceived destiny. After the war, in his 1920 State of the Union message to Congress, President Woodrow Wilson discussed the importance to the world of democracy. According to Wilson, "The Old World is just now suffering from a wanton rejection of the principle of democracy."[4] Wilson believed that the United States had an important role to play in protecting and promoting democracy around the world. The president went even further, however: He used the term *Manifest Destiny* to explain his vision of American leadership and involvement in world affairs. "It is surely the manifest destiny of the United States," Wilson declared, "to lead in the attempt to make this spirit prevail."[5] Although other American presidents did not cite Manifest Destiny as justification for their actions, the endurance of the idea that America has role and place as a world leader in the defense of freedom and democracy is undeniable.

Today, America's role as a superpower embodies many of these same elements of Manifest Destiny, including the desire to encourage the establishment of democratic governments around the world. John O'Sullivan and other nineteenth century expansionists might not recognize much of their world in modern-day America. They might, however, recognize the fruits of their labors and dreams to fulfill the Manifest Destiny of the United States.

CHRONOLOGY

1783   The Treaty of Paris ends the American Revolution.

1785   The Confederation Congress enacts the Land Ordinance, establishing the system of surveying western lands for settlement.

1787   The Confederation Congress enacts the Northwest Ordinance, banning slavery in the Northwest Territory.

1795   The United States and Spain sign Pinckney's Treaty, guaranteeing American rights to navigate the Mississippi River.

TIMELINE

1803
The United States doubles its territorial holdings when President Jefferson authorizes the acquisition of a vast amount of land west of the Mississippi River in the Louisiana Purchase

1820
Congress enacts the Missouri Compromise, prohibiting slavery north of the 36°30' parallel

1803 ──────────── 1823

1819
The United States receives Florida from Spain under the terms of the Adams-Onís Treaty

1823
The United States issues the Monroe Doctrine, ending European colonization in the Americas

1803   The United States doubles its territorial holdings when President Jefferson authorizes the acquisition of a vast amount of land west of the Mississippi River in the Louisiana Purchase.

1804–1806   Lewis and Clark lead the Corps of Discovery as they explore the northern portion of the Louisiana Territory.

1806–1807   Zebulon Pike leads an expedition that explores the southern portions of the Louisiana Territory.

1812   The United States declares war on Great Britain to protect American rights on the high seas.

1818–1819   The United States receives Florida from Spain under the terms of the Adams-Onís Treaty.

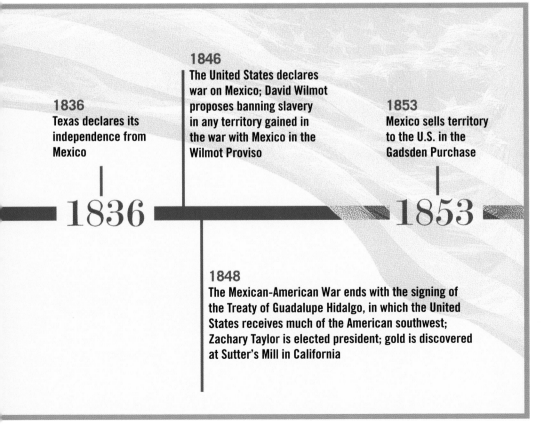

1836
Texas declares its independence from Mexico

1846
The United States declares war on Mexico; David Wilmot proposes banning slavery in any territory gained in the war with Mexico in the Wilmot Proviso

1853
Mexico sells territory to the U.S. in the Gadsden Purchase

1836   **1853**

1848
The Mexican-American War ends with the signing of the Treaty of Guadalupe Hidalgo, in which the United States receives much of the American southwest; Zachary Taylor is elected president; gold is discovered at Sutter's Mill in California

1820	Congress enacts the Missouri Compromise, prohibiting slavery north of the 36°30' parallel.
1823	The United States issues the Monroe Doctrine, ending European colonization in the Americas.
1836	Texas declares its independence from Mexico.
1844	James K. Polk is elected president.
1845	Florida is admitted to the Union; Texas is admitted to the Union.
1846	The United States declares war on Mexico; David Wilmot proposes banning slavery in any territory gained in the war with Mexico in the Wilmot Proviso.
1848	The Mexican-American War ends with the signing of the Treaty of Guadalupe Hidalgo, in which the United States receives much of the American southwest, including all or parts of what will become the states of California, Nevada, Utah, Arizona, Wyoming, Colorado, and New Mexico; Zachary Taylor is elected president; Gold is discovered at Sutter's Mill in California.
1850	California is admitted to the Union.
1853	Mexico sells additional territory to the United States in the Gadsden Purchase.
1854	The Kansas-Nebraska Act allows popular sovereignty to decide the question of slavery in the Kansas and Nebraska Territories.
1869	The first transcontinental railroad is completed.
1898	The United States fights and wins the Spanish-American War.
1917	The United States enters World War I.

NOTES

CHAPTER 1

1. Robert D. Sampson, *John O'Sullivan and His Times*. Kent, Ohio: Kent State University Press, 2003, 209.
2. The Avalon Project. Available online at http://www.yale.edu/lawweb/avalon/nworder.htm.
3. William W. Freehling, *The Road to Disunion: Secessionists at Bay 1776–1854*. Oxford: Oxford University Press, 1990, 461.
4. Michael A. Morrison, *Slavery and the American West: The Eclipse of Manifest Destiny and the Coming of the Civil War*. Chapel Hill, N.C.: University of North Carolina Press, 1997, 53.
5. Mason I. Lowance, ed., *A House Divided: The Antebellum Slavery Debates in America, 1776–1865*. Princeton, N.J.: Princeton University Press, 2003, 25.
6. Robert Walker Johannsen, *Stephen A. Douglas*. Champaign: University of Illinois Press, 1973, 227.

CHAPTER 2

1. John O'Sullivan, "Annexation," *United States Magazine and Democratic Review 17*, no.1 (July–August 1845): pp. 5–10. Available online at http://web.grinnell.edu/courses/HIS/f01/HIS202-01/Documents/OSullivan.html.
2. Robert J. Miller, *Native America, Discovered and Conquered*. Westport, Conn.: Praeger Publishers, 2006, 119.
3. Ibid.
4. Albert K. Weinberg, *Manifest Destiny: A Study of Nationalist Expansionism in American History*. Baltimore: Johns Hopkins Press, 1935, 145.
5. William Earl Weeks, *Building the Continental Empire: American Expansion from the Revolution to the Civil War*. Chicago: Ivan R. Dee., 1996, 60.
6. Frederick Merk, *Manifest Destiny and Mission in American History: A Reinterpretation*. New York: Alfred A. Knopf, 1963, 24.
7. Ernest Lee Tuveson, *Redeemer Nation: The Idea of America's Millennial Role*. Chicago: University of Chicago Press, 1968, 91.
8. Weeks, *Building the Continental Empire*, 61.
9. Reginald C. Stuart, *United States Expansionism and British North America, 1775–1871*. Chapel Hill: University of North Carolina Press, 1988, 85.
10. Ibid.
11. Weeks, *Building the Continental Empire*, 61.
12. Stuart, *United States Expansionism and British North America*, 85.
13. Grenville Kleiser, *Great Speeches and How to Make Them*.

Whitefish, Mont.: Kessinger Publishing Company, 2006, 181.

14. John Winthrop, "A Model of Christian Charity." Available online at http://religiousfreedom.lib.virginia.edu/sacred/charity.html.

15. Ibid.

16. Thomas Paine. *Common Sense.* Available online at http://www.gutenberg.org/dirs/etext94/comsn10.txt.

17. Ibid.

18. David S. Heidler and Jeanne T. Heidler, *Manifest Destiny.* Westport, Conn.: Greenwood Press, 2003, 2.

19. Walter A. McDougall, *Promised Land, Crusader State: The American Encounter with the World.* Boston: Houghton Mifflin Company, 1997, 78.

20. Weeks, *Building the Continental Empire*, 60–61.

21. Stuart, *United States Expansionism and British North America*, 1.

22. Weinberg, *Manifest Destiny*, 113.

23. Stuart, *United States Expansionism and British North America*, 81.

24. Weinberg, *Manifest Destiny*, 113.

25. Lars Schoultz, *Beneath the United States: A History of U.S. Policy Toward Latin America.* Cambridge: Harvard University Press, 1998, 24.

26. Weeks, *Building the Continental Empire*, 61.

CHAPTER 3

1. Saul K. Padover, *Jefferson.* Old Saybrook, Conn.: Konecky & Konecky, 1942, 135.

2. B.L. Rayner, *Sketches of the Life, Writings, and Opinions of Thomas Jefferson.* New York: A. Francis & W. Boardman, 1832, 430.

3. Weeks, *Building the Continental Empire*, 25.

4. Ibid.

5. Thomas Jefferson. Available online at http://etext.virginia.edu/jefferson/grizzard/johnson/johnson13.html.

CHAPTER 4

1. Scott Keller, *Marine Pride: A Salute to America's Elite Fighting Force.* New York: Citadel (Kensington Publishing Company), 2004, 88.

2. Weeks, *Building the Continental Empire*, 56.

3. Heidler and Heidler, *Manifest Destiny,* 73–74.

4. Weeks, *Building the Continental Empire*, 80.

5. Robert V. Remini, *Andrew Jackson and His Indian Wars.* Viking Penguin, 2001, 257.

6 "Northwest Ordinance; July 13, 1787," The Avalon Project at Yale Law School. Available online at http://www.yale.edu/lawweb/avalon/nworder.htm.

7. U.S. Constitution, Article IV, Section 3, Paragraph 2.

CHAPTER 5

1. Robert V. Hine and John Mack Faragher, *The American West: A New Interpretive History.* New Haven: Yale University Press, 2000, 160.

2. "Inaugural Address of James Knox Polk," The Avalon Project at Yale Law School. Available online at http://www.yale.edu/lawweb/avalon/presiden/inaug/polk.htm.

3. Ibid.

4. U.S. Constitution, Article II, Section 2, Clause 2.

CHAPTER 6

1. Alexis de Tocqueville, *American Institutions* (Henry Reeve, translator). Boston: Sever, Francis, and Co., 1870, 554–555.

2. http://www.humanitiesweb.org/human.php?s=h&p=c&a=q&ID=333.

CHAPTER 7

1. Allan Nevins, ed., *Polk: The Diary of a President, 1845–1849.* London: Longmans, Green and Co., 1952, 70.

2. "Message of President Polk," The Avalon Project at Yale Law School. Available online at http://www.yale.edu/lawweb/avalon/presiden/messages/polk01.htm.

3. Ibid.

4. Frederick Merk, *History of the Westward Movement.* New York: Knopf, 1978, 141.

5. Richard Worth, *Westward Expansion and Manifest Destiny in American History.* Berkeley Heights, N.J.: Enslow Publishers, 2001, 66.

CHAPTER 8

1. Quoted in Richard Worth, *Westward Expansion and Manifest Destiny in American History.* Berkeley Heights, NJ: Enslow Publishers, 2001, 66.

2. Howard Zinn, *A People's History of the United States* (1980), http://www.ditext.com/zinn/zinn8.html.

3. Ibid.

4. Morrison, *Slavery and the American West*, 71.

5. R.D. Monroe, "Congress and the Mexican War," Abraham Lincoln Historical Digitization Project. Available online at http://lincoln.lib.niu.edu/biography4text.html.

6. Peter F. Stevens, *The Rogue's March: John Riley and the St. Patrick's Battalion.* Herndon, Va.: Brassey's, 1999, 75.

7. "Lincoln's Spot Resolutions," National Archives and Records Administration–Records of the U.S. House of Representatives. Available online at http://www.lincolnbicentennial.gov/uploadedFiles/Learning_About_Lincoln/For_Teachers/Secondary/lincolns-spot-resolutions.pdf.

8. Thomas R. Hietala, *Manifest Design: Anxious Aggrandizement in Late Jacksonian America.* Ithaca, N.Y.: Cornell University Press, 1985, 240.

9. Morrison, *Slavery and the American West*, 71.

10. Merk, *Manifest Destiny and Mission in American History*, 107.

11. Ibid.

CHAPTER 9

1. "The Compromise of 1850," Digital History. Available online at http://www.digitalhistory. uh.edu/database/article_display. cfm?HHID=327.
2. Ibid.
3. Robert W. Johannsen et al. (Sam W. Haynes and Christopher Morris, eds.) *Manifest Destiny and American Antebellum Expansionism (Walter Prescott Webb Memorial Lectures).* College Station: Texas A & M University Press, 1997, 16.
4. Ibid.
5. Ibid.

BIBLIOGRAPHY

Brown, Charles H. *Agents of Manifest Destiny: The Lives and Times of the Filibusters.* Chapel Hill: University of North Carolina Press, 1980.

Burns, Edward McNall. *The American Idea of Mission: Concepts of National Purpose and Destiny.* New Brunswick, N.J.: Rutgers University Press, 1957.

Corps, Terry. *Historical Dictionary of the Jacksonian Era and Manifest Destiny.* Lanham, Md.: Scarecrow Press, 2006.

Freehling, William W. *The Road to Disunion: Secessionists at Bay, 1776–1854.* Oxford: Oxford University Press, 1990.

Graebner, Norman A., ed. *Manifest Destiny.* Indianapolis: Bobbs-Merrill Company, 1968.

Heidler, David S., and Jeanne T. Heidler. *Manifest Destiny.* Westport, Conn.: Greenwood Press, 2003.

Hietala, Thomas R. *Manifest Design: Anxious Aggrandizement in Late Jacksonian America.* Ithaca, N.Y.: Cornell University Press, 1985.

Hine, Robert V., and John Mack Faragher. *The American West: A New Interpretive History.* New Haven: Yale University Press, 2000.

Hofstadter, Richard. *The Paranoid Style in American Politics and Other Essays.* New York: Alfred A. Knopf, 1966.

Horsman, Reginald. *Race and Manifest Destiny: The Origins of American Racial Anglo-Saxonism.* Cambridge: Harvard University Press, 1981.

Johannsen, Robert W., et al. (Sam W. Haynes and Christopher Morris, eds.). *Manifest Destiny and American Antebellum*

Expansionism (Walter Prescott Webb Memorial Lectures). College Station: Texas A&M University Press, 1997.

Keller, Scott. *Marine Pride: A Salute to America's Elite Fighting Force.* New York: Citadel (Kensington Publishing Company), 2004.

Kleiser, Grenville. *Great Speeches and How to Make Them.* Whitefish, Mont.: Kessinger Publishing Company, 2006.

May, Robert E. *Manifest Destiny's Underworld: Filibustering in Antebellum America.* Chapel Hill: University of North Carolina Press, 2002.

McDougall, Walter A. *Promised Land, Crusader State: The American Encounter with the World.* Boston: Houghton Mifflin Company, 1997.

Merk, Frederick. *History of the Westward Movement.* New York: Knopf, 1978.

———. *Manifest Destiny and Mission in American History: A Reinterpretation.* New York: Alfred A. Knopf, 1963.

Morrison, Michael A. *Slavery and the American West: The Eclipse of Manifest Destiny and the Coming of the Civil War.* Chapel Hill: University of North Carolina Press, 1997.

Nevins, Allan, ed. *Polk: The Diary of a President, 1845–1849.* London: Longmans, Green and Co., 1952.

Padover, Saul K. *Jefferson.* Old Saybrook, Conn.: Konecky & Konecky, 1942.

Rayner, B.L. *Sketches of the Life, Writings, and Opinions of Thomas Jefferson.* New York: A. Francis & W. Boardman, 1832.

Remini, Robert V. *Andrew Jackson and His Indian Wars.* New York: Viking Penguin, 2001.

Sampson, Robert D. *John O'Sullivan and His Times.* Kent, Ohio: Kent State University Press, 2003.

Segal, Charles M., and David C. Stineback. *Puritans, Indians, and Manifest Destiny.* New York: G.P. Putnam's Sons, 1977.

Scholefield, Ethelbert O.S. *British Columbia from Earliest Times to the Present.* Vancouver, B.C.: S.J. Clarke, 1914.

Schoultz, Lars. *Beneath the United States: A History of U.S. Policy Toward Latin America.* Cambridge: Harvard University Press, 1998.

Smith, Gene A. *Thomas ap Catesby Jones: Commodore of Manifest Destiny.* Annapolis, Md.: Naval Institute Press, 2000.

Stevens, Peter F. *The Rogue's March: John Riley and the St. Patrick's Battalion.* Herndon, Va.: Brassey's, 1999.

Stuart, Reginald C. *United States Expansionism and British North America, 1775–1871.* Chapel Hill: University of North Carolina Press, 1988.

Tocqueville, Alexis de (Henry Reeve, translator). *American Institutions.* Boston: Sever, Francis, and Co., 1870.

Tuveson, Ernest Lee. *Redeemer Nation: The Idea of America's Millennial Role.* Chicago: University of Chicago Press, 1968.

Weeks, William Earl. *Building the Continental Empire: American Expansion from the Revolution to the Civil War.* Chicago: Ivan R. Dee, 1996.

Weinberg, Albert K. *Manifest Destiny: A Study of Nationalist Expansionism in American History.* Baltimore: Johns Hopkins Press, 1935.

Worth, Richard. *Westward Expansion and Manifest Destiny in American History.* Berkeley Heights, N.J.: Enslow Publishers, 2001.

FURTHER READING

Billington, Ray Allen. *Westward Expansion: A History of the American Frontier*. New York: Macmillan, 1974.

Collins, Jim. *Settling the American West*. New York: Franklin Watts, 1993.

Fehrenbach, T.R. *Lone Star: A History of Texas and the Texans*. New York: Macmillan, 1968.

Fresonke, Kris. *West of Emerson: The Design of Manifest Destiny*. Berkeley: University of California Press, 2003.

Lavender, David Sievert. *Westward Vision: The Story of the Oregon Trail*. New York: McGraw-Hill, 1963.

Pletcher, David M. *The Diplomacy of Annexation: Texas, Oregon, and the Mexican War*. Columbia: University of Missouri Press, 1975.

Schroeder, John H. *Mr. Polk's War: American Opposition and Dissent, 1846–1848*. Madison: University of Wisconsin Press, 1973.

Singletary, Otis A. *The Mexican-American War*. Chicago: University of Chicago Press, 1960.

Smith, Carter, ed. *Bridging the Continent: A Sourcebook on the American West*. Brookfield, Conn.: Millbrook Press, 1996.

Tibbitts, Alison Davis. *James K. Polk*. Berkeley Heights, N.J.: Enslow Publishers, 1999.

Vigness, David M. *The Revolutionary Decades: The Saga of Texas, 1810–1836*. Austin, Texas: Steck-Vaughn, 1965.

WEB SITES

Abraham Lincoln Historical Digitization Project: Congress and the Mexican War, 1844–1849

http://lincoln.lib.niu.edu/biography4text.html

The American Presidency Project: Woodrow Wilson, Eighth National Address, December 7, 1920

http://www.presidency.ucsb.edu/ws/index.php?pid=29561

***American Progress,* by John Gast**

http://memory.loc.gov/ammem/awhhtml/aw06e/d10.html

"Annexation," by John O'Sullivan

http://web.grinnell.edu/courses/HIS/f01/HIS202-01/Documents/OSullivan.html

***A People's History of the United States,* by Howard Zinn**

http://www.ditext.com/zinn/zinn8.html

The Avalon Project at Yale Law School: An Act to Organize the Territories of Nebraska and Kansas

http://www.yale.edu/lawweb/avalon/kanneb.htm

The Avalon Project at Yale Law School: Inaugural Address of James. Knox Polk

http://www.yale.edu/lawweb/avalon/presiden/inaug/polk.htm

The Avalon Project at Yale Law School: Louisiana Purchase Treaty, April 30, 1803

http://www.yale.edu/lawweb/avalon/diplomacy/france/louis1.htm

The Avalon Project at Yale Law School: Message of President Polk, May 11, 1846

http://www.yale.edu/lawweb/avalon/presiden/messages/polk01.htm

The Avalon Project at Yale Law School: Northwest Ordinance, July 13, 1787

http://www.yale.edu/lawweb/avalon/nworder.htm

Cambridge University Press: Excerpt from Amy S. Greenberg, *Manifest Manhood and the Antebellum American Empire*

http://assets.cambridge.org/97805218/40965/excerpt/
9780521840965_excerpt.pdf

Digital History: The Impending Crisis: The Compromise of 1850

http://www.digitalhistory.uh.edu/database/article_display.
cfm?HHID=327

Humanities Web: James K. Polk Quotations

http://www.humanitiesweb.org/human.
php?s=h&p=c&a=q&ID=333

Jefferson and His Colleagues

http://etext.virginia.edu/jefferson/grizzard/johnson/johnson13.
html

National Archives: "Teaching with Documents" Lincoln's Spot Resolutions

http://www.lincolnbicentennial.gov/uploadedFiles/Learning_
About_Lincoln/For_Teachers/Secondary/lincolns-spot-
resolutions.pdf

Project Gutenberg: Thomas Paine, *Common Sense*

http://www.gutenberg.org/dirs/etext94/comsn10.txt

Public Broadcasting Service: New Perspectives on the West: Antonio López de Santa Anna

http://www.pbs.org/weta/thewest/people/s_z/santaanna.htm

The Religious Freedom Page: We the People: A Model of Christian Charity, by Governor George Winthrop

http://religiousfreedom.lib.virginia.edu/sacred/charity.html

PHOTO CREDITS

INDEX

About the Author

DR. SHANE MOUNTJOY resides in York, Nebraska, where he is associate professor of history and dean of students at York College. Professor Mountjoy has received recognition from students and peers as an outstanding teacher. He has earned degrees from York College, Lubbock Christian University, the University of Nebraska, and the University of Missouri. He is the author of several books, including *The Battle of the Alamo* in the MILESTONES IN AMERICAN HISTORY series.